Ballads of the English Border.

BALLADS OF THE ENGLISH BORDER

By

Algernon Charles Swinburne

Edited with
Introduction, Glossary and Notes
by
WILLIAM A. MacINNES

LONDON:
WILLIAM HEINEMANN LTD.

First Printed, 1925.

Printed in Great Britain by Woods and Sons, Ltd., London, N. I.

CONTENTS

Introduction vii

The Ballads of the English Border .. xiii

Ballads, Ancient, Imitative and Modern 1

Notes to Ballads 229

Glossary.. 253

Bibliography 262

INTRODUCTION

THE English Borderland and more particularly Northumberland was first revealed to Swinburne when, as a child, he journeyed with his parents to Capheaton, the seat of his paternal grandfather. Many holidays were spent in this northern home and gradually the boy began to feel his young imagination fired by all the allurement of the Border country. In his daily rambles on foot, in his pony escapades over the moors, there rose before him the vision of an England of the past when feudal forts dotted the rugged landscape and escutcheoned knights rode forth to seek adventure. He grew to love the wooded hill slopes and the trackless wastes of gorseland that stretched far into the horizon with its distant rumble of a restless sea. And when, in later years, he thought of this part of England where

> " nought of Legend's dream
> Outshines the truth "

he found a secret pride in tracing his descent to an ancient Border clan of the Swinburnes, and even went so far as to characterise certain of his compositions as those of a Borderer.

While yet in his teens he became an ardent student of Northumbrian history which led him to investigate the wealth of local balladry, and this in turn opened up to his vista the more extensive field of Border folk-lore. In the pages of the " Minstrelsy " and the " Reliques " where Scott and Percy had gathered the gleanings of historical and popular song, Swinburne found a subject of strong appeal to his deep sense of poetic inspiration. His enthusiasm grew with his reading. From those authorities he passed to the collections of Kinloch, Jamieson, and Motherwell, only to find that much had yet to be discovered in the works of Buchan, Herd and the more obscure collectors of ancient rhymes. So proficient did he become through all this wide, intensive reading that many competent critics agreed with Rossetti in ranking Swinburne first among the authorities on the subject.

Such research, pursued with meticulous care, was not to prove unfruitful. From 1858 onwards, Swinburne had the definite aim in view of re-writing certain ballads and here he utilised every available version and shred of a theme. By skilful interpolation of stanzas from various renderings and by adding or substituting his own interpretation when necessary, he succeeded in reconstructing a number of ballads which could easily deceive the most sceptical critic of their authenticity. No one appreciated more fully this marvellous, assimilative talent of the poet than William Morris, himself a ballad-monger, when he wrote that if Swinburne were to introduce his own verses in a ballad they would be indistinguishable from the " original stuff." In these reproductions, as in his contemporary French work, Swinburne revealed a special and distinct province of his genius.

In the task of re-setting a ballad he combined a wealth of literary judgment with the finer qualities of poetical appreciation. Thus, in the many ballads and songs celebrating Hugh of Lincoln he gave careful consideration to all extant versions, from the earliest by Percy to those of Motherwell, Herd, and Brydges, not omitting the study of variants to be found in the pages of Jamieson, Michel, Hume, or Haliwell. From the first three he selected certain stanzas and reconstructing these into an harmonious whole, gave it the title of " The Jew's Daughter." In order to complete the work a critical note was added indicating the sources of study and including comparisons of different stanzas. Such is a typical example of the method adopted with most of the ballads contained in the first part of this volume, and it is worthy of note that the " Minstrelsy " of Scott appears to have been his chief work of reference, just as in his notes there is ample evidence of his indebtedness to the ballad collection of Professor Child.

Although it may seem at first to be merely a question of reconstruction, based on the collation of various texts, a comparison of Swinburne's version with others of the same ballad will prove that his debt to the former collectors was not so great as would appear. His method of punctuation differed from that of the stanzas he interpolated, and his spelling in dialect was not always in accordance with established practice. Even in his borrowings he did not hesitate to alter the order of certain words so as to suit his particular taste in verbal sonority and choice of vocabulary. Thus the individual touch of the master is evident in almost every verse of the ballad.

From such work Swinburne proceeded to the more ambitious and, at the same time, more difficult task of re-writing completely an old ballad, be it for the reason that he was not content with previous versions or that he simply wished to essay his skill in pastiches of ancient themes. "The Worm of Spindlestonheugh" offers a good example of this. The subject did not belong particularly to Border folk-lore but was a favourite in the ballad literature of Northern Europe. One version was printed by Hutchinson in 1776 and most probably Swinburne gained some suggestions from it as from others, but the ballad he composed bears little or no resemblance to any extant. The success of his venture, as Sir Edmund Gosse has pointed out, can only be properly appreciated by comparing the text here included with several of those in circulation during the last years of the 18th century. In the same way Swinburne took up the themes of "Lord Scales," "Earl Robert," "Duriesdike" and numerous other ballads.

From reconstruction and imitation the art of Swinburne passed to yet a third stage : that of the modern, refined version. This change in treatment was directly due to the influence of Dante Gabriel Rossetti whose counsel he highly valued and to whom, it appears, the ballads were recited. In the opinion of the Pre-Raphaelite poet the work of Swinburne in this sphere had hitherto been somewhat uncouth and lacked the delicacy of Victorian verse, although, in reality, its strong savour of northern dialect was more evocative of Border atmosphere than any of the so-called " modern " imitations of the time. Thus, in ballads such as "May Janet," "The King's Daughter," "The Brothers," etc., the theme was suggested to Swinburne perhaps by a title in the " Minstrelsy " or by a name common in balladry or even by a half-line of some Border song, and in such work the matter was entirely new while the chief aim was a judicious use of dialect in a setting more purely English. These last examples of the poet's skill demonstrate with what ease and felicity he could bring the Border ballad to meet the requirements of modern interpretation.

In anticipation of publishing the greater part of all this work Swinburne drafted a preface which, as it stands, is a disappointing introduction to so important a collection. It must be regarded, however, as incomplete. As with other projects of this period of feverish activity in drama, criticism, verse, and novel writing, that of a ballad collection never matured. The explanation may be traced partly to the fact that in 1857-8 Professor Child published his "English and Scottish Ballads," and that in 1858 and 1861 appeared Aytoun's "Ballads of Scotland," while in 1865 Allingham added yet another contribution to the list. As his bibliographer has suggested, Swinburne most probably abandoned his idea of a collection during the last months of 1861.

Although uncollected, certain ballads found their way into print. In 1862 Swinburne published for the first time one of his Border ballads ; two more were included in the " Poems & Ballads " of 1866, while in 1877 eight reached the stage of type in the galley-proofs of an unfinished novel " Lesbia Brandon." Another appeared in 1888 and in the following year those of 1877, with a few emendations in the text, supplemented the contents of the Third Series of " Poems & Ballads." Finally, in 1894, the poet decided to include in " Astrophel and other Poems," the remaining ballads which he wished to publish during his lifetime. After his death in 1909 some seventeen more were discovered and issued in limited editions for private circulation by Theodore Watts-Dunton and Thomas James Wise, with prefaces and prefatory notes contributed for the most part by Sir Edmund Gosse. Recent research has added a few others which, until now, have remained unpublished. With two or three exceptions the manuscripts of all the ballads are in the private Swinburnean collection of Thomas James Wise.

The present volume represents the composite work of Swinburne in Border balladry with the possible omission of what was said to have been destroyed by the poet himself. An arrangement of the contents into groups will show the three distinct stages of progress in this branch of the poet's art. In the first group are included the ballads which he has " reset," mainly by interpolation from different texts, and where, in his opinion, he has reconstructed a trustworthy version, as far as such is possible, of each ballad story. To the imitations comprising the second group are relegated those ballads in which the poet has treated a favourite Border theme in his own way without quotation from any anterior version. In such work Swinburne has carried the difficult art of successful pastiche to inimitable perfection. The modern ballads of the third group conclude the series and represent the last efforts in balladry of Swinburne, when, under Pre-Raphaelite influence, he introduced greater refinement in the choice both of subject and language.

Few poets or collectors have left to posterity so representative a series of ballads dealing with the English Borderland. In connection with certain of these, objection may be raised to their designation as " English," but this is precisely what Swinburne wished to emphasise. Indeed his introduction, despite its weak points, constitutes an effective reply to Andrew Lang's suggestion that poets south of the Tweed had better leave Scottish ballads alone. Swinburne was proud of the English ballad ; he championed its cause and sought to redeem its intrinsic value even at the expense of disparaging or attacking the northern usurpers of English song. To a certain extent he succeeded in retrieving a lost heritage ; his ingenuity and talent have contributed to enrich it in a volume where dialect, atmosphere and theme combine to evoke an almost forgotten age.

THE VICTORIA UNIVERSITY,
       MANCHESTER.   1924.

THE BALLADS OF THE ENGLISH BORDER

(Draft of a Preface by Swinburne)

THE most famous Scotchman of the last generation was fond
of quoting his master's inimitable and unanswerable query—
" Can you teach me how to jump off my own shadow ? " The
most illustrious Scotchman of all time bore evidence that he at
all events could not perform that feat, when he gave to one of
the most valuable books in our language the misleading and
indeed mendacious title—" Minstrelsy of the Scottish Border."
Even Sir Walter Scott—a name not less beloved of Englishmen
than of Scotchmen, and only less cherished than the name of
Shakespeare—could not jump off the shadow of his birth ;
could not, however unconscious and unsuspicious of any
lurking touch in his own noble nature of provincial vanity and
insincerity, be fair and honest, according to the limited lights
of English loyalty and veracity, when dealing with an apparently
debatable question between Scotland and England. It needs
no more acquaintance with the Borderland than may be gathered
from print by an English cockney or a Scotch highlander, to
verify the palpable and indisputable fact than even if England
can claim no greater share than Scotland in the splendid and
incomparable ballad literature which is one of the crowning
glories, historic or poetic, of either kingdom, Scotland assuredly
can claim no greater share in it than England : and that the
blatant Caledonian boobies whose ignorance is impudent
enough to question the claims of the English ballad—nay, even
to deny its existence, and consequently the existence of any
ballads dealing with any such unheard of heroes as Robin Hood,
Guy of Gisborne, Adam Bell, Clym o' the Cleugh, and William
of Cloudesley,—may be confuted and put to shame, if shame be

possible for such thick-skinned audacity to feel or understand, by the veriest smatterer who has an honest and intelligent eye in his impartial head. Quite as reasonably and quite as truthfully might Englishmen deny the existence of Scottish songs or ballads, and claim for their own country the parentage of all that glorious and spontaneous poetry which is, or should be, at this time of day the common pride and delight of us all; but Englishmen do nothing of the kind, and never did, and never will.

No man, I hope and believe, would have regarded any false and mean and malignant assumptions or impertinences, of which the baser sort among his scribbling countrymen might have been guilty, with more indignant and contemptuous disgust than Sir Walter Scott. But if—as seems only too certain—he did really cherish the envious provincial superstition that the Tweed rather than the Tyne or the Tees divided the native land of ballads from the land in which they are not indigenous, the retribution which befell his vain conceit was as perfect as Northumbrian devotion could have desired or Northumbrian humour could have devised. Surtees, not Scott, is the name of the one modern poet who has written ballads fit to be named and able to hold their own with all but the best of our ballads; no Scotchman—Scott of "Glenfinlas" or Leyden of "The Mermaid," or Hogg or Jamieson or Motherwell himself—has ever done that. And all the world knows how precious and unquestionable for antiquity were the ballads of Surtees in the eyes of Scott.

But this is of course a secondary, though of course a significant matter. What is not to be borne, and has been borne too long, is that English poems of immortal and incomparable beauty should be flaunted before the faces of Englishmen, as evidence of the fact that England is incapable and Scotland is capable of producing such work by spontaneous inspiration of impulse. It is impossible to distinguish by difference of dialect —transcribed or transcriptible—a poem born a little to the north or a little to the south of the Border. But if the evidence of locality is not to be accepted as sufficient, England might claim from Scotland that loveliest of all her numberless lovely songs, in which Arthur's Seat and St. Anton's Well are glorified beyond the glory of Helicon and Ida. It would be quite as fair and quite as reasonable to assume that this crowning flower of Scottish poetry belongs to England as to maintain that the finest of all ballads dealing with fairyland does not. At its opening, all maidens are forbidden, and for very sufficient reasons, " to come or gang by Carterhaugh." *

A. C. SWINBURNE.

[* In the MS. the following lines have been cancelled in pencil : "Now, if Carterhaugh is in Scotland, I'm a Scotchman : and, as Mr. Peggotty expresses it, 'I can't say no fairer than that.' The Young Tamlane, then, is as certainly and evidently an English ballad as Waly Waly is a Scottish song." A reference to Lockhart, v. 116, is inserted above the cancellation.—ED.]

CONTENTS OF BALLADS

I

THE DEMON LOVER	3
WALY, WALY	7
THE YOUNG TAMLANE	9
BONDSEY AND MAISRY	19
THE BONNY HYND	22
THE EARL OF ERROL	25
PROUD LADY MARGARET	29
THE JEW'S DAUGHTER	35
BONNIE BAHOME	38
JOHNIE OF BREADISLEE	42
YOUNG REDIN	47
THE CRUEL MOTHER	53
CHILDE WATERS	56
LIZIE WAN	63
THE QUEEN'S MARIE	65
WILLIE AND MAY MARGARET	69
LONG LONKIN	74
THE WATER O' WEARIE'S WELL	82
LORD THOMAS AND FAIR ANNIE	86
THE KEACH IN THE CREEL	92
THE KNIFE AND THE SHEATH	95
THE JOLLY BEGGAR	97
LORD DINGWALL	99

II

LADY ISABEL	107
WEARIESWA'	111
BURD MARGARET	120

CONTENTS

THERE GOWANS ARE GAY 126
LORD SCALES 128
DURIESDYKE 135
CLERK SAUNDERS 138
EARL ROBERT 141
THE TYNESIDE WIDOW 145
THE EARL OF MAR'S DAUGHTER 148
THE WORM OF SPINDLESTONHEUGH 152
WESTLAND WELL 161
LADY MAISIE'S BAIRN 165
THE WITCH MOTHER 167
LORD SOULIS 170
A LYKE-WAKE SONG 180
THE BRIDE'S TRAGEDY 181

III

THE BALLAD OF DEAD MEN'S BAY 189
THE KING'S DAUGHTER 194
THE SEA-SWALLOWS 197
A FRAGMENT OF A BORDER BALLAD 200
THE WEARY WEDDING 201
A REIVER'S NECK-VERSE 210
THE KING'S AE SON 211
MAY JANET 213
A JACOBITE'S FAREWELL 215
A JACOBITE'S EXILE 216
THE BLOODY SON 220
THE BROTHERS 224
BORDER BALLAD 227
THE WINDS 228

ANCIENT BALLADS

THE DEMON LOVER

"O WHERE have you been, my long, long love,
    This long seven years and more?"
"O I've come to seek my former vows
You granted me before."—

"O hold your tongue of your former vows,
For they will breed sad strife;
O hold your tongue of your former vows,
For I am become a wife."

He turned him right and round about
And the tear blinded his ee;
"I wad never hae trodden on Irish ground,
If it had not been for thee.

"I might have had a king's daughter,
Far, far beyond the sea;
I might have had a king's daughter
If it had not been for the love o' thee."—

"I despised the crown of gold,
The yellow silk also;
And I am come to my true love,
But wi' me she will not go."

"If ye might have had a king's daughter,
Yoursell ye hae to blame;
Ye might have taken the king's daughter,
For ye kent that I was nane."

"O false are the vows of womenkind,
But fair is their false body;
I wad never hae trodden on Irish ground,
If it had not been for the love o' thee.

"O what hae you to keep me wi',
If I should with you go?
If I would leave my husband dear,
My little young babes also?"—

"I hae seven ships upon the sea,
Laden wi' the finest gold;
And mariners to wait us upon;
All these you may behold."

"And I hae shoes for my love's feet,
Beaten o' the purest gold,
And lined wi' the velvet soft,
To keep my love's feet frae the cold."

She's tane up her little young babes,
Kissed them baith cheek and chin;
"O fare ye weel, my ain twa babes,
For I'll never see you again."

She set her foot upon the ship,
Nae mariners could she behold,
But the sails were of the taffetie
And the masts o' the beaten gold.

"O how do you love the ship," he said
"Or how do you love the sea?
Or how do you love the bold mariners
That wait upon thee and me?"

" O I do love the ship," she said,
And I do love the sea ;
But woe be to the dim mariners
That nowhere I can see."

They had not sailed a league, a league,
A league but barely three,
When dismal grew his countenance
And drumlie grew his ee.

They had not sailed a league, a league,
A league but barely three,
Until she espied his cloven foot
And wept right bitterly.

" O hold your tongue of your weeping," he says,
" Of your weeping now let me be ;
I will shew you how the lilies grow
On the banks of Italy."—

" O what hills are yon, yon pleasant hills,
That the sun shines sweetly on ? "
" O yon are the hills of heaven," he said,
" Where you will never win."—

" O whatten a mountain is yon," she said,
" All so dreary wi' frost and snow ? "
" O yon is the mountain of hell," he said,
" Where you and I will go."

And aye when she turned her round about,
Aye taller he seem'd for to be ;
Until that the tops o' that gallant ship,
Nae taller were than he.

He strak the tapmast wi' his hand,
The foremast wi' his knee ;
And he brake that gallant ship in twain,
And sank her in the sea.

WALY, WALY

O WALY, waly up the bank,
  And waly, waly down the brae,
And waly, waly by yon burn side,
Where I and my love wont to gae.
I set my back intill an aik,
I thought it was a trusty tree;
But first it bowed, and syne it brak,
Sae my true love did lightly me.

O waly, waly, gin love be bonny,
A little time while it is new;
But when it's auld, it waxeth cauld,
And fades away like morning dew.
O wherefore should I busk my head?
Or wherefore should I kame my hair?
For my true love has me forsook,
And say's he'll never love me mair.

Now Arthur's Seat shall be my bed,
The sheets shall neer be filed by me;
Saint Anton's well shall be my drink,
Since my true love's forsaken me.
Martinmas wind, when wilt thou blaw,
And shake the green leaves aff the tree?
O gentle death, when wilt thou come?
For of my life I am wearie.

" Tis not the frost that freezes fell,
Nor blawing snaw's inclemencie ;
'Tis not sic cauld that makes me cry,
But my love's heart grown cauld to me.
When cockle shells turn siller bells,
When mussels grow on every tree,
When frost and snaw shall warm us a'
Then shall my love prove true to me.

When we came in by Glasgow town
We were a comely sight to see ;
My love was clad i' the black velvet,
And I mysell in cramasie.
When we came in by Edinburgh
We were a fair sight to behold ;
My love was clad in cramasie
And I mysell in the beaten gold.

But, had I wist, before I kissed,
That love had been sae ill to win,
I had locked my heart in a kist o' goud,
And pinned it with a siller pin.
Oh !   Oh ! if my young babe were born,
And set upon the nurse's knee,
And I mysell were dead and gone !
For a maid again I'll never be.

THE YOUNG TAMLANE

"O I forbid ye, maidens a',
    That wear gowd on your hair,
To come or gang by Carterhaugh,
For young Tamlane is there.

" There's nane that gaes by Carterhaugh,
But maun leave him a wad ;
Either gowd rings or green mantles,
Or else their maidenhead.

" Now gowd rings ye may buy, maidens,
Green mantles ye may spin ;
But gin ye lose your maidenhead,
Ye'll ne'er get that again."

But up then spak her, fair Janet,
The fairest of a' her kin ;
" I'll come and gang by Carterhaugh,
And ask nae leave o' him."

Janet has kilted her green kirtle,
A little abune her knee ;
And she has braided her yellow hair,
A little abune her bree.

And when she came to Carterhaugh,
She gaed beside the well ;
And there she fand his steed standing,
But away was himsell.

She hadna pu'd a rose, a rose,
A rose baith red and green ;
When by it came him, young Tamlane,
Says—" Lady, let abene.

" What gars ye pu' the rose, Janet ?
What gars ye break the tree ?
Or why come ye to Carterhaugh
Withouten leave o' me ? "

Says—" I will pu' the rose, the rose,
And I will break the tree ;
I'll come and gang to Carterhaugh,
And ask nae leave o' thee."

He's tane her by the milk-white hand,
Amang the roses green ;
He's laid her low on good green leaves,
A' for her body's seen.

He's tane her by the milk-white hand
Amang the roses red ;
He's laid her low on fair flowers,
To take her maidenhead.

When she came to her father's court,
She looked pale and wan ;
They thought she'd dreed some sair sickness,
Or been wi' some leman.

She didna comb her yellow hair
Nor make mickle of her head ;
And ilka thing that lady took,
Was like to be her dead.

It's four and twenty ladies fair
Were playing at the ba';
Janet, the wightest of them anes,
Was faintest o' them a'.

Four and twenty ladies fair
Were playing at the chess;
And out there came the fair Janet,
As green as any grass.

Out and spak an auld grey-headed knight,
Lay ower the castle wa';
"And ever, alas! for thee, Janet,
But we'll be blamed a.'"

"Now haud your tongue, ye auld grey knight,
And an ill dead may ye die;
Father my bairn on whom I will,
I'll father nane on thee."

And then spak her father dear,
And he spak meek and mild,
"And ever, alas! my sweet Janet,
I hear ye gae with child."

"And if I be with child, father,
Mysell maun bear the blame;
There's ne'er a knight about your ha'
Shall hae the bairnie's name.

"If my love were an earthly knight,
As he's an elfin grey,
I wadna gie my ain true love
For nae lord that ye hae."

She's prinked hersell and prinn'd hersell
By the ae light of the moon,
And she's away to Carterhaugh,
To speak wi' young Tamlane.

And when she came to Carterhaugh,
She gaed beside the well;
And there she saw the steed standing,
But away was himsell.

She hadna pu'd a rose, a rose,
Nor broken a branch but ane,
Till by it came him, young Tamlane,
Says—"Lady, let alane.

"O why pu' ye the pile, Janet,
The pile o' the gravel green,
And a' to kill the bonny bairn,
That we got us between?"

"O why pu' ye the pile, Janet,
The pile o' the gravel grey,
And a' to kill the bonny bairn
That we got in our play?

"For if it be a knave bairn
He's heir of a' my land;
But if it be a lass bairn
In red gowd she shall gang.

"The truth ye'll tell to me, Tamlane,
A word ye maunna lie;
Gin e'er ye was in holy chapel,
Or sained in Christentie?"

" The truth I'll tell to thee, Janet,
A word I winna lie ;
A knight me got and a lady me bore,
As well as they did thee.

" Roxburgh was a hunting knight,
And loved hunting well,
As I rode east and west yon hill,
This ill thing me befell.

" Roxburgh was my grandfather,
Took me with him to ride ;
And as we frae the hunting came
This harm did me betide.

" There came a wind out o' the north
A sharp wind and a well ;
And drowsy, drowsy as I was,
Down frae my horse I fell.

" The Queen of Fairies keppit me
In yon green hill to dwell ;
Then wad I never tire, Janet,
In Elfish land to dwell.

" But aye, at every seven year's end
They pay the teind to hell ;
And I am sae fat and fair of flesh,
I fear 'twill be mysell.

" The night is Hallowe'en, Janet,
The morn is Hallowday,
And they that will their true love win
They have sma' time to stay.

" The night it is good Hallowe'en,
When fairy folk will ride ;
Thro' England and thro' a' Scotland
And thro' the world wide.

" O they begin at sky-setting
Ride a' the evening tide ;
And she that will her true love borrow
At Miles Cross maun him bide."

" But how shall I thee ken, Tamlane,
Or how shall I thee knaw,
Amang so many unearthly knights,
The like I never saw ? "

" Ye'll do ye down to Miles Cross
Between twae' hours and ane,
And full your hand o' holy water,
And cast your compass roun'.

" The first company that passes by,
Say na, and let them gae ;
The next company that passes by,
Say na, and do right sae ;
The third company that passes by,
Then I'll be ane o' thae.

" The firsten court that comes you till
Is published king and queen ;
The neisten court that comes you till
It is maidens mony ane.

" First let pass the black, Janet,
And syne let pass the brown ;
But grip ye to the milk-white steed,
And pu' the rider down.

" For I ride on the milk-white steed,
A gowd star on my crown ;
Because I was a christened knight
They gave me that renown.

" They'll turn me in your arms, Janet,
An adder and an ask ;
They'll turn me in your arms, Janet,
A bale that burns fast.

" They'll turn me in your arms, Janet,
A red-hot gad of airn ;
But haud me fast, let me not pass,
And I'll father your bairn.

" They'll turn me in your arms, Janet,
Like iron in strong fires ;
But haud me fast, let me not pass,
And ye'll have your desires.

First dip me in a stand o' milk,
And then in a stand o' water ;
But haud me fast, let me not pass,
I'll be your bairn's father.

They'll turn me in your arms, Janet ;
Like to a silken string ;
But haud me fast, let me not pass,
Till ye see the fair morning.

" They'll turn me in your arms, Janet,
A tod but and an eel ;
But haud me fast, let me not pass,
As you do love me weel.

" They'll turn me in your arms, Janet,
A dove but and a swan ;
They'll turn me in your arms, Janet,
A mother-naked man ;
But haud me fast, let me not pass,
I'll be myself again."

Then she has done her to Miles Cross
Between twae hours and ane ;
She's filled her hands o' holy water,
And cast her compass roun'.

About the dead hour o' the night,
She heard the bridles ring ;
And Janet was as glad o' that,
As any earthly thing.

The firsten court that came her till
Was published king and queen ;
The neisten court that came her till
Was maidens mony ane.

And first gaed by the black, black steed,
And syne gaed by the brown ;
She gripped her to the milk-white steed,
And pu'd the rider down.

She's tane the horse then by the head,
And loot the bridle fa' ;
And up there raise an erlish cry,
" He's won amang us a' ! "

He grew into her arms two
An esk but and an adder ;
She held him fast, let him not pass,
He was her bairn's father.

He grew into her arms two,
An adder and a snake ;
She held him fast, let him not pass,
He was her world's make.

He grew into her arms two,
Like iron in strong fire ;
She held him fast, let not him pass,
And she gat her desire.

He grew into her arms two,
Like to a silken string ;
She held him fast, let him not pass,
Till she saw fair morning.

He grew into her arms two,
A dove but and a swan ;
He grew into her arms two
A mother-naked man ;
She held him fast, let him not pass,
And sae her true love wan.

Out then spak the Queen o' Fairies
Out of a bush of broom ;
" She that hath gotten young Tamlane
Has gotten a stately groom."

Out then spak the Queen o' Fairies,
Out of a bush of rye ;
" She's tane awa the bonniest knight
In a' my companie."

"But had I kenn'd, Tamlane," she says,
" A lady wad borrowed thee,
I wad tane out thy twa' grey een,
Put in twa een o' tree.

" Had I but kenn'd Tamlane," she says,
" Before ye came frae hame,
I wad tane out your heart o' flesh,
Put in a heart o' stane."

" Had I but had the wit yestreen
That I hae coft the day.
I'd paid my kane seven times to hell
Or you'd been won away.

BONDSEY AND MAISRY

O COME along wi' me, brother,
  Now come along wi' me;
And we'll gae seek our sister Maisry
Into the water o' Dee.

The eldest brother he steppit in,
He steppit to the knee;
Then out he jumped upo' the bank,
Says, " This water's nae for me."

The second brother he steppit in,
He steppit to the quit;
Then out he jumped upo' the bank,
Says, " This water's won'rous deep."

The third brother he steppit in,
He steppit to the chin;
Out he gat and forward wade,
For fear o' drowning him.

The youngest brother he steppit in,
Took his sister by the han';
Says, " Here she is, my sister Maisry,
Wi' the honey draps on her chin.

" O if I were in some bonny ship,
And in some strange countrie,
For to find out some cunning man
To gar Maisry speak to me!"

Then out it speaks an auld woman,
A laidly thing to see;
Says—" Let the salt upon her mouth
And the bread upon her knee;
And take a sprinkle o' the wan water
And shed it abune her ee."

" The night it is her low lykewake,
The morn her burial day;
And ye maun watch at mirk midnight
To hear what she will say."

About the middle o' the night
The cocks began to craw;
And at the dead hour o' the night
The corpse began to thaw.

" O sister, tell me who is the man,
That did your body win?
And likewise who is the evil man
That threw you in the linn?"

" O Bondsey was the only man
That did my body win;
And likewise Bondsey was the man
That threw me in the linn."

" O will we Bondsey head, sister,
Or will we Bondsey hang?
Or will we set him at our bow end,
Let arrows at him gang?"

" Ye winna Bondsey head, brothers,
Nor will ye Bondsey hang;
But ye'll pike out his twa grey een,
Make Bondsey blind to gang."

" Ye'll put to the gate a chain of gold,
A rose garland gar make ;
And ye'll put that on Bondsey's head,
A' for your sister's sake."

THE BONNY HYND

O MAY she comes, and May she goes,
　　Down by yon gardens green;
And there she spied a gallant squire
　　As squire had ever been.

And May she comes, and May she goes,
　　Down by yon hollin tree;
And there she spied a brisk young squire
　　And a brisk young squire was he.

"Give me your green mantle, fair maid,
　　It's no for you a weed;
Gin ye winna give me your green mantle,
　　Give me your maidenhead."

He's tane her by the milk-white hand
　　And saftly laid her down;
And when he's lifted her up again,
　　He's gien her a siller comb.

"Perhaps there may be bairns, kind sir,
　　Perhaps there may be nane;
But if you be a courtier
　　You'll tell me soon your name."

"I am nae courtier, fair maid,
  But new come frae the sea;
I am nae courtier, fair maid,
  But when I court wi' thee.

"They call me Jock, when I'm abroad,
  Sometimes they call me John;
But when I'm in my father's bower
  Jock Randal is my name."

"Ye lee, ye lee, ye bonny lad,
  Sae loud's I hear ye lee;
For I'm Lord Randal's ae daughter,
  He has nae mair nor me."

"Ye lee, ye lee, ye bonny May
  Sae loud's I hear ye lee;
For I'm Lord Randal's ae ae son
  Just new come ower the sea."

She's putten her hand down by her gare
  And out she's tane a knife;
She's soaked it in her bonny heart's blood
  And twined herself o' life.

And he has tane up his bonny sister,
  Wi' the saut tear in his een;
And he has buried his bonny sister
  Amang the hollins green.

And syne he's hied him ower the dale
  His father dear to see;
"Sing Oh! and Oh! for my bonny hynd,
  Beneath yon hollin tree!"

"What needs you care for your bonny hynd,
    For it you needna care;
Take you the best, gie me the warst,
    Since plenty is to spare."—

"I carena for your hynd, my lord,
    I carena for your fee;
But Oh! and Oh! for my bonny hynd,
    Beneath the hollin tree!"

"O were ye at your sister's bower,
    Your sister fair to see,
You'll think nae mair o' your bonny hynd
    Beneath the hollin tree."

THE EARL OF ERROL

O ERROL'S place is a bonny place,
   It stands upon yon plain;
The flowers on it grow red and white,
The apples red and green.

The raubing o't and the daubing o't
According as ye ken;
The thing we ca' the daubing o't
Is—Errol's no a man!

O Errol's place is a bonny place,
It stands upon yon plain;
But what's the use of Errol's place,
He's no like other men?

As I came in by yon canal
And by yon bowling-green,
I might have pleased the best Carnegie
That ever bore the name.

As sure as your name is Kate Carnegie
And mine is Gibbie Hay,
I'll gar your father sell Kinnaird
Your tocher for to pay.

To gar my father sell his land
Wad it not be a sin,
To tocher ony weary dwarf
That canna tocher win?

Now she is on to Edinburgh
A' for to try the law,
And Errol he has followed her
His manhood for to shaw.

What needs me wash my apron
Or dry ot upon a door?
What needs me eke my petticoat
Hings even down before?

What needs me wash my apron
Or hing it upon a pin?
For lang will I gang but and ben
Or I hear my young son's din.

Then out it spak her sister,
Whose name was Lady Anne;
Had I been Lady Errol, she says,
Or come of Errol's clan,
I wad not in this public way
Have shamed my ain gudeman.

* * * * *

But Errol got it in his mind
To choice a maid himsell;
And he has tane a weel-faured may
Came in her milk to sell.

Look up, look up, my weel-faured may,
Look up and think no shame;
I'll gie to thee five hunder mark
To bear to me a son.

He took her by the milk-white hand
And led her up the green ;
And twenty times he kissed her mouth
Before his lady's een.

When they were laid in the proof bed
And a' the lords looking on,
Then a' the fifteen vowed and swore
That Errol was a man.

He kept her there into a room
Three quarters of a year,
And when the nine lang months were out
A braw young son she bare.

And there was three thairbut, thairbut,
And there was three thairben,
And three looking ower the window-lin,
Crying " Errol's proved a man ! "

And when the word gaed thro' the town
A cry the sentry gae ;
O fair befa' you, Errol, now,
For you have won the day.

O I'll tak off my robes of silk
And fling them ower the wa',
And I'll gae maiden hame again ;
Awa', Errol, awa' !

Tak hame your daughter, Sir Carnegie,
And put her till a man,
For Errol cannot please her
Nor nane o' Errol's men.

And ilka day the plate was laid,
But and a siller spune ;
And three times cried ower Errol's yetts—
Lady Errol, come and dine.

The raubing o't and the daubing o't,
According as ye ken,
The thing they ca' the daubing o't . . .
Lady Errol lies her lane.

PROUD LADY MARGARET

I T was a sad and a rainy night
   As ever rained frae town to town ;
Lady Margaret looked ower her castle wa'
Beheld the fields sae brown.

She was looking ower her castle high
To see what might her fa' ;
And there she saw a grieved ghost
Coming walking ower the wa'.

" O are you a man o' mean," she says,
Seeking ony o' my meat ?
Or are you a rank robber
Comin' my bower to break ? "

" O I am neither a man o' mean
Nor yet a robber lown ;
But I am a bonny kind squire
Rides in the fields sae brown.

" A bed, a bed, now, Lady Margaret,
A bed, a bed, let me lie down ;
For I am sae wet and sae weary
I canna gang a ride frae town."

29

"You seem to be no gentleman,
You wear your boots sae wide,
You seem to be some cunning hunter,
You wear the horn so side."

"I am nae cunning hunter," he says,
"Nor sic I seem to be;
But I am come to this castle
A' for the love of thee;
And if ye winna grant me love,
My time is come that I maun die."

"If ye should die for me the night
Few for you will make meen;
For mony gude lord's done the same,
Their graves are growing green."

"O I'll put smiths in your smithy
To shoe for you a steed;
And I'll put tailors in your bower
To shape to you a weed.

"I will put cooks in your kitchen
And butlers in your ha';
And on the top o' your father's castle
I'll ligg good corn and saw."

"If ye be some bonny kind squire
As I trust not ye be,
Ye'll answer to me some three questions
That I shall ask at thee.

"Now what is the flower, the ae first flower,
Springs either on moor or dale?
And what is the bird, the bonny bonny bird,

Sings next the nightingale?
And what is the finest thing," she says,
" That king or queen can wale? "

" The primrose is the ae first flower,
Springs either on moor or dale;
And the thristlecock is the sweetest bird
Sings next the nightingale;
And yellow gowd is the finest thing
That king or queen can wale."

" And what's the little coin," she says,
" Wad buy my castle bound?
And what's the little boat," she says,
" Can sail the world all round? "

" O hey, how mony sma' pennies
Make thrice three thousand pound?
Or hey, how mony sma' fishes
Swim a' the salt sea round? "

" Mony's the questions I've speired at thee
And ye've shewn me monything;
But what is the seemliest light you'll see
Into a May morning? "

" Berry brown ale in a birken spale
And wine in a horn green;
A milkwhite lace in a fair maids' dress
Looks gay in a May morning."

" Ye've speired mony things at me, Lady,
And I've answered them a';
Ye are mine and I am thine
Among the sheets sae sma'."

"I think ye maun be my match," she said,
"My match and something mair;
There was never man gat sic a grant
Out of my father's heir.

"My father was lord of nine castles,
My mother lady of three;
My father was lord of nine castles,
And there's nane to heir but me.

"And round about a' thae castles
You may both plough and saw;
And on the fifteenth day of May
The meadow they will maw."

"O haud your tongue, Lady Margaret," he says,
"For loud I hear you lie;
Your father was lord of nine castles,
Your mother was lady of three;
Your father was lord of nine castles,
But ye fall heir to but three.

"And round about a' thae castles
You may baith plough and sae;
But on the fifteenth day of May
The meadows will not maw.

"I am your brother Willie," he says
I trow ye kenna me;
I am Willie your ae brither
Was far ayont the sea."

"Gin ye be Willie my ae brither,
This mickle marvels me;
O wherein is your bonny arm,
Ye were wont to clip me wi'?"

" By worms they're eaten ; in mools they're rotten ;
Behold, Margaret, and see ;
And mind, for a' your mickle pride,
Sae shall become o' thee."

" Gin ye be Willie, my ae brither,
Fu' sair this marvels me ;
O wherein is your bonny lip,
Ye were wont to kiss me wi' ? "

" By worms they're eaten, in mools they're rotten ;
Behold, Margaret, and see ;
And mind, for a' your mickle pride,
Sae will become o' thee."

" Gin ye be Willie, my ae brither,
As I doubt sair ye be,
I'll draw to me my gowd cleiding,
And gang the night wi' thee.

" O haud your tongue, Lady Margaret," he says,
" Again I hear you lie :
For ye've unwashen hands and ye've unwashen feet,
To gang to-day wi' me.

" My body is buried in Dumferline
And far ayont the sea,
There's nae rest in my body, Margaret,
A' for the pride o' thee.

" Leave off your pride, Lady Margaret," he says,
" Use it not ony mair,
For if ye come where I have been,
The wreak of it maun be sair.

" Cast off, cast off, Lady Margaret," he says,
The gowd lace frae your crown ;
For if ye come where I have been
Ye'll wear it lower down.

" When ye're set in the goodly kirk,
The gowd kills on your hair,
There is nae lady that sees your face
But wishes your pains were sair.

" And when ye walk in the good kirk-yard
Wi' the gold your gowns between,
There is nae lady that looks you upon
But wishes your grave were green.

" But the wee worms are my bedfellows
And cauld clay is my sheet ;
And where the weary winds do blow
My body lies and sleeps."

34

THE JEW'S DAUGHTER

THE rain rins doun through Mirryland toun,
  Sae does it doun the Pa';
Sae does the boys of Mirryland toun
When they play at the ba'.

They toss the ball so high, so high,
They toss the ball so low;
They toss the ball in the Jew's garden
Where the Jews are sitting arow.

Then out and came the Jew's daughter,
Clothed all in green;
"Come hither, come hither, my pretty Sir Hugh,
And fetch your ball again."

"I durst not come, I durst not go,
Without my schoolfellows a';
For gin my mither should chance to know
She wad gar my blood to fa'".

"Come up, sweet Hugh, come up, dear Hugh,
Come up and speak to me,"
"I mayna came, I winna come,
Without my bonny boys three."

She's tane her to the Jew's garden
Where the grass grew lang and green;
She pulled an apple red and white
To wile the bonny boy in.

She's wiled him in through ae chamber,
She's wiled him in through twa ;
She's wiled him in tell her ain chamber,
The flower out ower them a'.

And she's tane out a little penknife ;
Hung low down by her gair ;
She's twined the young thing of his life,
A word he never spak mair.

And first came out the thick, thick blood
And syne came out the thin ;
And syne came out the bonny heart's blood,
There was nae mair within.

She laid him on a dressing-board
And dressed him like a swine ;
Says—" Lie ye still there, my bonny Sir Hugh,
Wi' your apples red and green."

She rowed him in a cake of lead,
Says—" Lie ye there and sleep ; "
She cast him in the Jew's draw-well,
Was fifty fathom deep.

When bells were rungen and mass was sungen,
And a' the bairns came hame,
Then ilka lady had her young son,
But Lady Helen had nane.

She row'd her mantle her about,
And sair sair gan she weep :
And she ran into the Jew's castle,
When they were all asleep.

" My bonny Sir Hugh, my pretty Sir Hugh,
I pray thee to me speak "
" O lady, rin to the deep draw-well,
Gin ye your son would seek."

Lady Helen ran to the deep draw-well,
And knelt upon her knee ;
" My bonny Sir Hugh, if ye be here,
I pray thee speak to me."

" Oh, the lead it is wondrous heavy, mither,
The well it is wondrous deep ;
The little penknife sticks in my throat,
And I downa to ye speak."

" Gae hame, gae hame, my mither dear,
Fetch me my windling sheet ;
And at the back of Mirryland toun
It's there we twa shall meet."

O the broom and the bonny, bonny broom,
The broom that makes full sore ;
A woman's mercy is very little,
But a man's mercy is more.

BONNIE BAHOME

Lord Thomas and Lady Maisry
  Were both born at one birth ;
There was mair love between thae twa
Than there was in a' the earth.

Lord Thomas and Lady Maisry
Were both born in one hour ;
There was mair love between thae twa
Than either in hall or bower.

Lord Thomas and Lady Maisry
They were both born in one bed ;
There was mair love between thae twa
Than a rose has leavis red.

Lord Thomas and Lady Maisry
They were born of mothers twain ;
But they twa bairns were laid together,
Thereof they were full fain.

Lord Thomas and Lady Maisry
In one robe they were clad ;
There was a good time them between,
Thereof they were full glad.

It fell out upon a day
Lord Thomas he thought lang ;
And he's deep sworn upon a book
That to Bonny Bahome he would gang.

Lady Maisry beheld upon his ship,
Stood low down by the sea ;
Says—" Wae be to you, sails and tackling.
Took Lord Thomas from me."

Lady Maisry beheld upon his men,
Stood low down by the sand ;
Says—" Wae be to you, ye weary mariners,
Took Lord Thomas from land."

She thought her love had been on sea
Far ower against Bahome ;
But he was still in a quiet chamber,
Hearing his lady's moan.

" Now peace, now peace, thou Lady Maisry,
And I pray thee moan not so ;
For I am deep sworn upon a book
That to Bonny Bahome I must go."

She's gien him a chain o' the beaten gowd
And a ring with a rubis red ;
Says—" While this chain is on your body,
Your blood shall never be shed.

" And ye'll ken gin the stanes be fallen out
Or gin the gowd ring break,
That my thought is never on Clerk Thomas,
But on another make."

He hadna been in Bonnie Bahome
A twelve-month and a day,
When he beheld upon his ring,
That the stanes were fallen away.

" O whatten a weird is this weary weird,
A weary thing to dree?
For the stones that were of the royal red
They are grown grey to me.

" Ye'll take my riches that's in Bahome,
And deal them liberally,
To the young that canna, the auld that manna,
The blind that downa see.

" Ye'll take red gowd to my burying
And deal it out of hand,
To a young maid's wedding and a young bairn's cledding
That can neither go nor stand.

" And ye maun deal for a burying dole
My lands that are to gie,
To women that are in strong travailing,
Can neither fight nor flie.

" And ye maun bid to my burying
Three and three and three;
The auld that canna, the young that shanna,
The sick that winna lang be."

His lady stood at a little shatwindow,
Beheld baith sea and side;
And she thought lang for Clerk Thomas,
Her love was ill to bide.

She's reached her head out ower the stane,
Beheld the leas of land;
" I would my new love were clad in clay,
My auld love at my hand."

She's leaned her ower the castle wa',
Beheld baith water and wide ;
Her thought was a' for Clerk Thomas,
In heart is not to hide.

She's laid her chin out ower the stane,
That weary water to see ;
" I would my new love were borne on a bier
And my auld love back to me.

" But ye maun buy me a goodly ship,
A goodly ship to me,
And I will sail to Bonny Bahome,
That good lord for to see."

When she came to Bonnie Bahome,
Saw mony that wrung their hands ;
" I'm feared it's mony unco lords
Having my love to the sands."

As she came by my good lord's bower,
Saw mony black steeds and brown ;
" I'm feared it's mony unco lords
Having my love from town."

As she came by my good lord's bower,
Saw mony black steeds and grey ;
" I'm feared it's mony unco lords
Having my love to the clay."

JOHNIE OF BREADISLEE

JOHNIE rose up in a May morning,
   Called for water to wash his hands ;
   " Gar loose to me the good grey dogs
That are bound wi' iron bands."—

When Johnie's mother gat word o' that,
Her hands for dule she wrang ;
" O Johnie, for my benison,
To the Greenwood dinna gang.

" Eneugh ye hae of good wheat bread
And eneugh o' the blood-red wine ;
And, therefore, for nae venison, Johnie,
I pray thee, stir frae hame."

But Johnie's busk'd up his good hand bow,
His arrows ane by ane,
And he is gone to Durrisdeer
To ding the dun deer down.

As he came down by Merrimass
And in by the benty line
There has he espied a deer lying
Aneath a bush of ling.

Johnie lookit east, and Johnie lookit west,
And a little below the sun ;
And there he spied the dun deer sleeping
Aneath a bush of broom.

Johnie shot, and the dun deer lap,
And he wounded her on the side ;
But atween the water and the brae
His hounds they laid her pride.

And Johnie has brittled the deer sae weel
That he's had out her liver and lungs ;
And wi' these he has feasted his bloody hounds,
As if they had been earl's sons.

They ate sae much o' the venison
And drank sae much o' the blood ;
That Johnie and a' his bloody hounds
Fell asleep as they had been dead.

And by there came a silly auld carle,
An ill death mote he die !
For he's awa' to Hislinton
Where the seven foresters did lie.

" What news, what news, my silly auld man,
What news bring ye to me ? "
" Nae news, nae news," said the silly auld man,
" But what mine een did see.

" As I came in by Merrimass
And down amang the scrogs,
The bonniest child that ever I saw
Lay sleeping amang his dogs.

" The shirt that was upon his back
Was o' the Holland fine ;
The doublet which was over that
Was o' the Lincome twine.

" The buttons that were on his sleeve
Were o' the gowd sae good;
The good grey hounds he lay amang,
Their mouths were dyed wi' blood."—

Up bespak the first forester,
The first forester of a';
" Gin this be Johnie of Breadislee,
It's time we were awa'."—

Up bespak the neist forester,
The neist forester of a' :—
" Gin this be Johnie of Breadislee
To him we winna draw."—

But up bespak the sixth forester,
His sister's son was he;
" Gin this be Johnie of Breadislee,
We soon shall gar him die."—

They have ridden ower muir amd moss
Till they came to yon bush of scrogs,
And then to yon wan water
Where he slept amang his dogs.

The first shot that they did shoot,
Wounded Johnie abune the knee;
And out and spak the seventh forester,
" The neist will gar him die."

" Wae be to you, foresters,.
And an ill death may ye die !
For there is not a wolf in a' the wood
Would have done the like to me."

Johnie's set his back against an aik,
His foot against a stane ;
And he has slain the seven foresters,
He has slain them a' but ane.

He has broke three ribs in that ane's side,
But and his collar bane ;
He's laid him twafald ower his steed,
Bade him carry the tidings hame.

" There is not a bird in a' this forest
Will do as mickle for me,
As dip its wing in the wan water,
And streek it on my eebree."

" Aft have I tane to my mither
The dun deer and the roe ;
But now I'll take to my mither
Much sorrow and much woe."

" Aft have I tane to my mither
The dun deer and the hare ;
But now I'll take to my mither
Much sorrow and much care."

" O is there na a bonny bird
Can sing as I can say,
Could flee away to my mither's bower
And tell to fetch Johnie away ? "—

The starling flew to his mither's window stane,
It whistled and it sang ;
And aye the ower word o' the tune
Was " Johnie tarries lang."

They made a rod o' the hazel bush,
Another o' the slae-thorn tree,
And mony mony were the men
At fetching ower Johnie.

Then out and spak his auld mither
And fast her tears did fa' ;
" Ye wadna be warned, my son Johnie,
Frae the hunting to bide awa'.

" Aft have I brought to Breadislee
The less gear and the mair,
But I ne'er brought to Breadislee
What grieved my heart sae sair.

" But wae betide that silly old carle,
An ill death shall he die !
For the highest tree in Merrimass
Shall be his morning's fee."

Now Johnie's good hand bow is broke,
And his good grey dogs are slain ;
And his body lies dead in Durriesden
And his hunting it is done.

YOUNG REDIN

" O LADY rock never your young son young
      One hour langer for me ;
For I have a sweetheart in Garlioch Wells
I love far better than thee.

" The very sole o' that lady's foot
Than thy face is far more white."—
" But nevertheless now, young Redin,
Ye will bide in my bower a' night " ?

When he was in her arms laid
And giving her kisses sweet,
Then out she's tane a little penknife
And wounded him sae deep.

Then up and spake the popingay
That flew abune her head ;
" Keep well, keep well your green cleiding
From ae drap of his bleid."

" O I'll keep well my green cleiding
From ae drap of his bleid,
Better than I'll keep thy clattering tongue
That prattles in thy head.

" O lang, lang is the winter night
And slowly daws the day ;
There is a slain knight in my bower
And I wish he were away."

47

Then up bespak her bower-woman,
And she spak aye wi' spite ;
" Gin there be a slain knight in your bower
It's yoursell that hae the wyte."

" Heal well, heal well, ye May Catherine,
Heal well this deed on me ;
The silks that were drapen for me gin . . .
They shall be sewed for thee."

" O I hae healed on my mistress
A twelve-month and a day ;
And I hae healed on my mistress
Mair than I can say."

They hae booted him and spurred him
As he was wont to ride ;
A hunting horn tied round his waist,
A sharp sword by his side;

And they hae had him to the wan water,
For a' men call it Clyde,
The deepest spot in Clyde's water,
There they flang him in
And put a turf on his breast-bane
To haud young Redin down.

Syne up bespak the wily parrot,
As he sat on the brier ;
" Gae hame, gae hame, ye Lady Maisry,
And pay your maiden's hire."

" Come down, come down, ye wily parrot,
Come down into my hand ;
Your cage shall be o' the beaten gowd,

Where now it's but the wand.
For ae gowd feather that's in your wing
I wad gi' a' my land."

" I winna come down, I canna come down,
I winna come down to thee ;
For as ye've done to young Redin,
Ye'll do the like to me ;
Ye'll thraw my head off my breast-bane
And throw me in the sea."

O there came seekin' young Redin
Many a lord and knight ;
And there cam seekin' young Redin
Mony a lady bright.

And out it speaks the little young son,
Sat on the nurse's knee ;
" It fears me sair of young Redin
He's in bower wi' yon lady."

Then they hae called her, May Catherine,
And she swore by the thorn,
That she saw not him, young Redin,
Sin' yesterday at morn.

Then they hae called her, Lady Maisry,
And she sware by the moon,
That she saw not him, young Redin,
Sin' yesterday at noon.

" But ye'll seek Clyde's water up and down,
Ye'll seek it out and in ;
It fears me sair o' Clyde's water
That he is drowned therein."

Then up bespak young Redin's mither
And a dowie woman was she ;
" There is not a ford in Clyde's water
But my son wad gae through."

" Gar douk, gar douk, the King he cried,
Gar douk, for gowd or fee ;
O wha will douk for young Redin,
Or wha will douk for me ? "

They douked in thro' the wan burn-bank
Sae did they out thro' the other ;
" We can douk nae mair for young Redin,
Altho' he were our brother."

Then out and spak the popinjay
That flew abune their head ;
" Dive on, dive on, ye divers a'
It's there they've made his bed."

" But ye'll leave aff your day diving
And ye'll dive in the night ;
The pot that young Redin lies in
The Candles they'll burn bright.

" There are twa ladies in yon bower
And even in yon ha',
And they hae killed him, young Redin,
And casten him awa'.

" They booted him and spurred him
As he was won't to ride ;
A hunting-horn tied round his neck
A sharp sword by his side.

"The deepest pot o' Clyde's water,
There they flang him in;
Laid a turf on his breast-bane
To haud young Redin down."

They left off their day-diving
And they dived on the night;
The pot that young Redin lay in,
The candles were burning bright.

The deepest pot in Clyde's water.
They fand young Redin in;
A green turf on his breast-bane
To haud young Redin down.

O white, white were his wounds washen,
As white as a linen clout;
But as that lady came him near
His wounds they gushed out.

"It's surely been my May Catherine,
O ill may her betide;
I ne'er wad slain him, young Redin,
And thrown him in the Clyde."

The King he called his hewers a'
To hew down wood and thorn,
For to put up a strong bale-fire
The bower-woman to burn.

And they hae tane her, May Catherine,
And they hae putten her in;
It took na on her cheek, her cheek,
It took na on her chin.

But it sang the points of her yellow hair
For healing the deadly sin,
And they hae tane her, Lady Maisry,
And they hae putten her in;

It took upon her cheek, her cheek,
It took upon her chin;
It sang the point of her yellow hair—
She burned like keckle-pin.

THE CRUEL MOTHER

IT fell ance upon a day, Edinboro', Edinboro',
It fell ance upon a day, Stirling for aye,
It fell ance upon a day,
The clerk and lady went to play,
Sae proper Saint Johnston stands fair upon Tay.

If my baby be a son, Edinboro', Edinboro',
If my baby be a son, Stirling for aye,
If my baby be a son,
A web of gowd to put him on,
Sae proper Saint Johnston stands fair upon Tay.

If my baby be a maid wean, Edinboro', Edinboro',
If my baby be a maid wean, Stirling for aye,
If my baby be a maid wean,
A web of red to hap her in,
Sae proper Saint Johnston stands fair upon Tay.

She's leaned her back against the wa', Edinboro', Edinboro',
She's leaned her back against the wa', Stirling for aye,
She's leaned her back against the wa'
Pray'd that her pains might fa',
Sae proper Saint Johnston stands fair upon Tay.

She's leaned her back against the thorn, Edinboro', Edinboro',
She's leaned her back against the thorn, Stirling for aye,
She's leaned her back against the thorn,
There she has her two babes born,
Sae proper Saint Johnston stands fair upon Tay.

O bonny baby, if ye suck sair, Edinboro', Edinboro',
O bonny baby, if ye suck sair, Stirling for aye,
O bonny baby, if ye suck sair,
Ye'll never suck by my side mair,
Sae proper Saint Johnston stands fair upon Tay.

She's riven the muslin frae her head, Edinboro', Edinboro',
She's riven the muslin frae her head, Stirling for aye,
She's riven the muslin frae her head,
Tied the babies hand and feet,
Sae proper Saint Johnston stands fair upon Tay.

O smile na sae, my bonny babe, Edinboro', Edinboro',
O smile na sae, my bonny babe, Stirling for aye,
O smile na sae, my bonny babe,
Gin ye smile sae sweet ye'll smile me dead,
Sae proper Saint Johnston stands fair upon Tay.

She's ta'en out her little penknife, Edinboro', Edinboro',
She's ta'en out her little penknife, Stirling for aye,
She's ta'en out her little penknife,
Twined the young things of their life,
Sae proper Saint Johnston stands fair upon Tay.

She's howked a hole anent the meen, Edinboro', Edinboro',
She's howked a hole anent the meen, Stirling for aye,
She's howked a hole anent the meen,
There she's laid her sweet babies in,
Sae proper Saint Johnston stands fair upon Tay.

She's had her to her father's ha', Edinboro', Edinboro',
She's had her to her father's ha', Stirling for aye,
She's had her to her father's ha',
She was the meekest maid amang them a',
Sae proper Saint Johnston stands fair upon Tay.

As she looked ower the castle wa', Edinboro', Edinboro',
As she looked ower the castle wa', Stirling for aye,
As she looked ower the castle wa',
She saw twa bonnie boys playing at the ba',
Sae proper Saint Johnston stands fair upon Tay.

" O bonny babies, gin ye were mine, Edinboro', Edinboro',
O bonny babies, gin ye were mine, Stirling for aye,
O bonny babies, gin ye were mine,
Ye should wear the silk and the sabelline,
Sae proper Saint Johnston stands fair upon Tay."

" O wild mother, when we were thine, Edinboro', Edinboro',
O wild mother, when we were thine, Stirling for aye,
O wild mother, when we were thine,
To us ye werena half sae kind,
Sae proper Saint Johnston stands fair upon Tay.

But now we're in the heavens high, Edinboro', Edinboro',
But now we're in the heavens high, Stirling for aye,
But now we're in the heavens high,
And ye've the pains of hell to try,
Sae proper Saint Thomas stands fair upon Tay."

CHILDE WATERS

CHILDE Waters stood in his fair stable
And stroked his milk-white steed;
To him there came the fairest lady
That ever wore woman's weeds.

Says, " Christ you save, good Childe Waters "
Says, " Christ you save and see;
My girdle of gold that was too long,
Is now too short for me.

" And all is with one child of yours,
I feel stir at my side;
My gown of green it is too strait,
Before it was too wide."

" If the child be mine, fair Ellen," he said,
" Be mine as you tell me,
Then take you Cheshire and Lancashire both,
Take them your own to be.

" If the child be mine, fair Ellen," he said,
" Be mine as you would swear,
Then take you Cheshire and Lancashire both
And the child to be your heir."

She says, " I had rather have one kiss,
Childe Waters, of your mouth;
Than I would have Cheshire and Lancashire both
That lie by north and south.

" And I had rather have one twinkling,
Childe Waters, of thine ee,
Than I would have Cheshire and Lancashire both,
To take them my own to be."

" To-morrow, Ellen, I must forth ride
Far into the north country ;
The fairest lady that I can find,
Ellen, must go with me."

" And ever I pray you, Childe Waters,
Your foot page let me be."

" If you will my foot page be, Ellen,
As you do tell to me,
Then you must cut your gown of green,
An inch above your knee.

" So must you do your gown of green
An inch above your ee ;
You must tell no man what is your name,
My foot page then you shall be."

She all the long day Childe Waters rode
Ran barefoot by his side,
Yet was he never so courteous a knight,
To say, " Ellen, will you ride ? "

She all the long day Childe Waters rode
Ran barefoot through the broom ;
Yet was he never so courteous a knight,
To say, " Put on your shoon."

" Ride softly," she said, " O Childe Waters,
Why do you ride so fast ?

The child, which is no man's but thine,
My body it will brast."

He saith—" Seest thou yon water, Ellen,
That flows from bank to brim ? "
" I trust in God, O Childe Waters,
You never will see me swim."

But when she came to the water-side
She sailed to the chin ;
" Now the Lord of heaven be my speed,
For I must learn to swim."

The salt waters bare up her clothes,
Our Lady bare up her chin ;
Childe Waters was a woe man, good Lord,
To see fair Ellen swim.

And when she over the water was,
She stood against his knee ;
He said, " Come hither, thou fair Ellen,
Lo yonder what I see.

" Seest thou not yonder hall, Ellen,
Of red gold shines the gate ?
Of twenty-four fair ladies there,
The fairest is my mate.

" Seest thou not yonder Hall, Ellen,
Of red gold shines the tower ?
There are twenty-four fair ladies there,
The fairest is my paramour."

" I see the hall now, Childe Waters,
Of red gold shines the gate ;

God give you joy now of yourself,
And of your worldly mate.

" I see the hall now, Childe Waters,
Of red gold shines the tower ;
God give you good now of yourself,
And of your paramour."

There twenty-four fair ladies were
A playing at the ball,
And Ellen, the fairest lady there,
Must bring his steed to the stall.

There twenty-four fair ladies were
A playing at the chess,
And Ellen, the fairest lady there,
Must bring his horse to grass.

And then bespake Childe Waters' sister,
These were the words said she ;
" You have the prettiest page, brother,
That ever I did see ;

" But that his belly it is so big,
His girdle stands so high ;
And ever, I pray you, Childe Waters,
Let him in my chamber lie."

" It is not fit for a little footpage,
That has run thro' moss and mire,
To lie in the chamber of any lady
That wears so rich attire.

" It is more meet for a little footpage,
That has run thro' moss and mire,
To take his supper upon his knee,
And lie by the kitchen fire."

Now when they had supped every one
To bed they took their way;
He said, " Come hither, my little foot-page,
And hearken what I say.

" Go thee down into yonder town,
And low into the street;
The fairest lady that thou canst find,
Hire in mine arms to sleep;
And take her up in thine arms twain,
For filing of her feet."

Ellen is gone into the town
And low into the street;
The fairest lady that she could find
She hired in his arms to sleep;
And took her up in her arms twain
For filing of her feet.

" I pray you now, good Childe Waters,
Let me lie at your feet;
For there is no place about this house,
Where I may say a sleep."

Between his feet and the lady's feet
Over the bed she lay;
And the night went on between them twain,
Till it was near the day.

He said. " Rise up, my little footpage,
Give my steed corn and hay;

And give him now the good black oats
To carry me better away."

Up then rose she, fair Ellen,
And gave his steed corn and hay ;
And so did she the good black oats,
To carry him the better away.

She leaned her back to the manger side
And grieviously did groan ;
She leaned her back to the manger side
And there she made her moan.

And that beheard his mother dear
She heard her bitter woe ;
She said, " Rise up, thou Childe Waters,
And into thy stable go.

" For in thy stable is a ghost,
That grieviously doth groan ;
Or else some woman labours with child,
She is so woe-begone."

Up then rose Childe Waters soon,
And did on his shirt of silk ;
And then he put on his other clothes
On his body as white as milk.

And when he came to the stable door,
Full still he there did stand,
That he might hear her, fair Ellen,
How she made her monand.

She said, " Lullaby, mine own dear child,
Lullaby, dear child, dear ;
I would thy father were a king
Thy mother laid on a bier."

" Peace now," he said, " good Fair Ellen,
Be of good cheer, I pray ;
And the bridal and the churching both
Shall be upon one day."

LIZIE WAN

Lizie Wan sits at her father's bower door
  Weeping and making a mane;
And by there came her father dear;
" What ails thee, Lizie Wan? "

" I ail, and I ail, dear father," she said
" And I can shew you why;
There is a child between my twa sides
Between my dear billie and I."

Now Lizie Wan sits at her father's bower door
Sighing and making a mane;
And by there comes her brother dear,
" What ails thee, Lizie Wan? "

" I ail, I ail, dear brother," she said,
" And I can shew you why;
There is a child between my twa sides
Between you, dear billie and I."

" And hast thou told father and mother o' that,
And hast thou told sae o' me? "
And he has drawn his good braid sword
That hung down by his knee.

And he has cutted off Lizie Wan's head
And her fair body in three;
And he's awa' to his mother's bower,
And sair aghast was he.

" What ails thee, what ails thee, Geordie Wan,
What ails thee so fast to run ?
For I see by thy ill colour
Some fallow's deed thou's done."

" Some fallow's deed I have done, mither,
And I pray you pardon me ;
For I've cutted off my greyhound's head
He wadna rin for me."

" Thy greyhound's blood was never sae red,
O my son, Geordie Wan ;
For I see by thy ill colour
Some fallow's deed thou's done."

" Some fallow's deed I hae done, mither,
And pray you pardon me ;
For I hae cutted off Lizie Wan's head
And her fair body in three."

" O, what will thou do when thy father comes hame,
O my son, Geordie Wan ? "
" I'll set my foot in a bottomless boat
And swim to the sea ground."

" And when will thou come hame again,
O my son, Geordie Wan ? "
" The sun and the moon shall dance on the green
That night when I come hame."

THE QUEEN MARIE

MARIE Hamilton's to the kirk gane
  Wi' ribbons in her hair ;
The king thought mair o' Marie Hamilton
Than of a' the ladies there.

Marie Hamilton's to the kirk gane
Wi' ribbons at her briest ;
The king thought mair o' Marie Hamilton
Than he listened to the priest.

Marie Hamilton's to the kirk gane
Wi' gloves upon her hands ;
The king thought mair o' Marie Hamilton
Than the queen and a' her lands.

She hadna been about the king's court
A month but barely ane,
Till she was beloved by a' the king's court
And the king the only man.

She hadna been about the king's court
A month but barely three,
Till frae the king's court Marie Hamilton,
Marie Hamilton durstna be.

The king is gone to the abbey garden
To pull o' the saim tree,
To scale the babe frae Marie's heart,
But the thing it wadna be.

O she has row'd it in her apron
And set it on the sea;
" Gae sink ye or swim ye, bonny babe,
Ye'll get nae mair o' me."

Word is to the kitchen gone,
And word is to the ha',
And word is to the noble room
Amang the ladies a'
That Marie Hamilton's brought to bed
And the bonny babe's missed and awa'.

Queen Marie came tripping down the stairs
Wi' the gold rings in her hair;
" O where is the little babe " she says,
That I heard greet sae sair? "

" O no, O no, my noble queen,
Think nae sic thing to be;
It was but a stitch into my side
And sair it troubles me."

" Get up, get up, Marie Hamilton,
Get up and follow me;
For I am going to Edinburgh Town,
A rich wedding for to see."

O slowly, slowly raise she up
And slowly put she on;
And slowly rode she out the way
Wi' mony a weary groan.

The queen was clad in scarlet,
Her merry maids all in green;
At every town that they came to
They took Marie for the queen.

" Ride hooly, hooly, gentlemen,
Ride hooly now wi' me !
For never, I am sure, a wearier burd
Rade in your companie."—

But little wist Marie Hamilton
When she rade on the brown
That she was going to Edinburgh Town
And a' to be put down.

" What need ye heck ! and how ! ladies ?
What need ye how for me ?
Ye never saw grace at a graceless face,
Queen Marie had nane to gie."

When she gaed up the Tolbooth stairs
The corks frae her heels did flie ;
And long e'er she cam down again
She was condemned to die.

When she cam to the Netherbow port
She laughed loud laughters three ;
When she cam to the gallows foot
The tears blinded her ee.

" Yestreen the Queen had four Maries,
The night she'll hae but three,
There was Marie Seaton, and Marie Beaton,
And Marie Carmichael, and me."

" Often have I dressed my queen
And put gold upon her head ;
But now I've gotten for my reward
The gallows tree to tread."

" Often have I dressed my queen
And put gold upon her hair ;
But now I've gotten to my reward
The gallows to be my share.

" O ye Mariners, mariners, mariners,
That sail upon the sea,
Let neither my father nor mother get wit
This dog's death I'm to die."

" I charge ye all, ye mariners,
That sail out ower the faem,
Let neither my father nor mother get wit,
But that I'm coming hame."

" For if my father and mother get wit
And my bauld brethen three,
O mickle wad be the good red blood
This day wad be spilt for me ! "

" O little did my mother ken,
The day she cradled me,
The lands I was to travel in
Or the death I was to die ! "

WILLIE AND MAY MARGARET

"GIE corn to my horse, mither,
    Gie meat unto my man;
For I maun gang to Margaret's bower,
I'll win ere she lie down."

" O bide this night wi' me, Willie,
O bide this night wi' me ;
The besten cock of a' the nest
It your supper shall be."

" A' your cocks and a' your nests,
I value not a prin ;
For I maun gang to May Margaret's bower,
I'll win ere she lie down."

" Stay this night wi' me, Willie,
O stay this night wi' me ;
The besten sheep in a' the flock
It your supper shall be."

" A' your sheep and a' your flocks
I value not a prin ;
For I maun gang to May Margaret,
I'll win ere she lie down."

" O gin ye gang to May Margaret
Sae sair against my will,
The deepest pot in Clyde's water
I give ye to won intill."

"The good steed that I ride upon
Cost me thrice thretty pound;
And I'll put trust in his swift feet,
To have me safe to land."

As he rade ower yon high, high hill,
And down yon dowie den,
The noise that was in Clyde's water
Wad feared five hundred men.

"O roaring Clyde, ye roar ower loud,
Your streams seem wondrous strang;
Make me your wreck as I come back
But spare me as I gang."

Then he is on to May Margaret's bower
And tirled at the pin;
"O sleep ye, wake ye, Margaret," he said,
"Ye'll open and let me in."

"O wha is this at my bower door,
That calls me by my name?"
"It is your first love, sweet Willie,
This night newly come hame."

"I hae few lovers thereout, thereout,
As few have I therein;
The besten love that ever I had
Was here but late yestreen."

"The warsten stable in a' your stables
For my puir steed to stan';
The warsten bower in a' your bowers
For me to lie therein;
My boots are fu' o' Clyde's water,
I'm shivering at the chin."

"My barns are fu' o' corn, Willie,
My stables are fu' o' hay;
My bowers are fu' o' gentlemen,
They winna be gone till day."

"O fare ye weel then, May Margaret,
Sin' better maunna be;
I've getten my mother's malison
Coming this night to thee."

As he rade ower yon high, high hill
And down yon dowie den;
The rushing that was in Clyde's water
Took Willie's wand frae him.

He leaned him ower his saddle-bow
To win his wand again;
The rushing that was in Clyde's water
Took Willie's hat frae him.

He leaned him ower his saddle-bow,
To win his hat wi' force;
The rushing that was in Clyde's water
Took Willie frae his horse.

His brither stood upon the bank,
Says "Fie, man, will ye drown?
Ye'll turn ye to your high horse head
And ye'll learn how to sowm."

"How can I turn to my horse head
And how can I learn to sowm?
I've getten my mither's malison
And it's here that I maun drown."

71

And down it's sunken him, sweet Willie,
Into the pot sae deep,
And up it's waken'd her, May Margaret,
Out of her drowsy sleep.

" Come hither, come hither, lady, my mither,
And read this dreary dream;
I dream'd my love was at our gates,
And nane wad let him in."

" Lie still, lie still now, May Margaret,
Lie still and take your rest;
Sin' your true love was at your gates,
It's but twa quarters past."

Nimbly, nimbly raise she up,
And nimbly pat she on;
And aye the higher she cried on Willie,
The louder blew the win'.

The firsten step that she steppid in
She steppid to the queet;
" And ever alas ! " quo' that lady,
" This water's wondrous deep."

The neisten step that she wade in
She wadit to the knee;
Quo' she, " I could wade further in
Gin my love I could see."

The neisten step that she wade in
She wadit to the chin;
The deepest pot in Clyde's water
She gat sweet Willie in.

" You've had a cruel mither, Willie,
And I have had anither ;
But we shall sleep in Clyde's water
Like sister and like brither."

LONG LONKIN

Lonkin was as gude a mason
    As ever built wi' stane;
He built Lord Wearie's castle,
But wages gat he nane.

"O pay me now, Lord Wearie,
O pay me now my fee."
"I canna pay you, Lonkin,
Till I be back from sea."

"O pay me now, Lord Wearie,
O pay me out of hand."
"I canna pay you, Lonkin,
Till I be back to land."

The lord said to his lady
As he mounted his horse,
"Beware of Long Lonkin
That lies in the moss."

The lord said to his lady
As he rode away,
"Beware of Long Lonkin
That lies in the clay."

"What care I for Lonkin
Or any of his kin?
My doors are all shut
And my windows penned in."

There were six little windows
And they were all shut,
But one little window
And that was forgot.

But one little window
Was loose in the pin;
And at that little window
Long Lonkin crept in.

" Where's the lord o' this house ? "
Says the Lonkin;
" He's ower the sea,"
Says Orange to him.

" Where's the men o' this house ? "
Says the Lonkin;
" They're at the barn threshing,"
Says Orange to him.

" Where's the maids o' this house ? "
Says the Lonkin;
" They're at the well washing,"
Says Orange to him.

" Where's the bairns o' this house ? "
Says the Lonkin;
" They're at the school reading,"
Says Orange to him.

" Where's the son o' this house ? "
Says the Lonkin;
" He's awa' to buy pearlins
Gin our lady lie in."

" Then she'll never wear them,"
Says the Lonkin ;
" And that is nae pity,"
Says Orange to him.

" Where's the lady o' this house ? "
Says the Lonkin ;
" She's in her bower sleeping,"
Says Orange to him.

" How shall we get her down ? "
Says the Lonkin ;
" Prick the babe in the cradle,"
Says Orange to him.

" That wad be a pity,"
Says the Lonkin ;
" Nae pity, nae pity,"
Says Orange to him.

Lonkin's tane a sharp knife
Hung down by his gair,
And he's gien the bonny babe
A sharp wound and a sair.

Long Lonkin he rocked
And Orange she sang,
Till frae ilka pore o' the cradle
The red blood out sprang.

Then out spak the lady
As she stood on the stair,
" What ails my bairn, Orange,
That he's greeting sae sair ?

"O still my bairn, Orange,
O still him wi' the pap."
"He winna still, lady,
For this nor for that."

"O still my bairn, Orange,
O still him wi' the kame."
"He winna still, lady,
Till his father be hame."

"O still my bairn, Orange,
O still him wi' the ring."
"He winna still, lady,
For ony kin' o' thing."

"O still my bairn, Orange,
O still him wi' the keys."
"He winna still, lady,
Nor yet he winna please."

"O still my bairn, Orange,
O still him wi' the knife."
"He winna still, lady,
Gin I'd lay down my life."

"O still my bairn, Orange,
O still him wi' the wand."
"He winna still, lady,
For a' his father's land."

"O still my bairn, Orange,
O still him wi' the bell."
"He winna still, lady,
Till ye come down yoursell."

"O how can I come down
This bitter cauld night
Without ever a coal,
Or a clear candle-light ? "

"There's twa' smocks in your coffer
As white as a swan's,
Put ane o' them about you
It will shew you light down."

The firsten step she steppit
She steppit on a stane ;
The neisten step she steppit,
She met the Lonkin.

"O mercy now, Long Lonkin,
Have mercy upon me ;
Tho' you've tane my young son's life
Mysell you may let be."

"Shall I kill her, Orange,
Or shall I let her be ? "
"O kill her, kill her, Lonkin,
For she ne'er was good to me."

"Hold the gold basin
And make it fair and clean ;
Hold the gold basin
For your heart's blood to run in."

"To see my bairn's heart blood
It grieves me fu' sair ;
To haud my ain heart's blood
It grieves me mickle mair."

" Hold the gold basin
And scour it out and in ;
Hold the gold basin
For your Mother's blood to rin."

" To hold the gold basin
Fu' sair it grieves me ;
O kill me, dear Lonkin,
And let my mother be."

" Hold the basin, maidens,
And make it fu' clean,
Hold the gold basin
For your lady's blood to rin."

" To hold the gold basin
It makes us full woe ;
O kill us, dear Lonkin,
And let our lady go."

" Hold the basin, Orange,
And scour it out and in ;
Hold the gold basin
For your lady's blood to rin."

" To hold the gold basin
It makes me fu' fain ;
To hold my lady's heart's blood
It is but little pain."

" She's none of my comrades,
She's none of my kin ;
To hold my lady's heart's blood
It is but little sin."

79

"O lacked ye your meat, Orange,
Or lacked ye your fee,
Or lacked ye for onything
A fair lady could gie?"

"I lacked for nae meat, lady,
I lacked for nae fee;
But I lacked for a hantle
A fair lady could gie."

"And they've tane this lady,
They've tied her wi' bands,
And in her sweet heart's blood
They twa have dipt their hands.

The lord sat over sea
Drinking the wine;
"I wish a' may be weel
With a' things of mine."

"I wish a' may be weel
Wi' my lady at hame,
For the rings of my fingers
Are bursten in twain."

And ere three months were out
Lord Wearie cam again;
The firsten step he steppit
He was right full of pain.

"O wha's blood is this
That lies in the cham'er?"
"It is your lady's heart's blood;
It is as clear as lammer."

" And wha's blood is this
That lies in my ha' ? "
" It is your young son's heart's blood,
It is the clearest of a'."

O sweet sang the blackbird
That sang but ower the tree ;
But sairer grat Lonkin
When he was boun' to die.

O bonny sang the mavis,
That sang ower the brake,
But sairer grat Orange
When they tied her to the stake.

THE WATER O' WEARIE'S WELL

THERE came a bird out of a bush
    On water for to dine;
And sighing sair, says the king's daughter,
" O waes this heart o' mine ! "

He's taken a harp intill his hand,
He's harped them all asleep;
Except it was the king's daughter,
Ae wink she couldna get.

He's courted her but and he's courted her ben,
He's courted her into the ha',
Till he gat the good will of May Colvin
To mount and ride awa'.

She's gane to her father's coffers
Where a' the fair gowd lay;
And she's taken the red and she's left the white
And she's gane lightly away.

She's gane down to her father's stable
Where a' his horse did stand;
And she's taken the best and she's left the warst
That was in her father's land.

He's loupen on the foremost steed,
Tane her on behind himsell;
And they baith rade down to that water
That they ca' Wearie's Well.

" Wide in, wide in, my fair lady,
For here is nought to dwell;
O mony's the time I've watered steeds
Wi' the water o' Wearie's Well.

The first step that she stepp't in
She steppit to the knee;
And sighing sair says May Colvin,
" This water's nae for me."

" Wide in, wide in, now, May Colvin
For here ye maunna dwell;
O mony's the time I've watered steeds
Wi' the water o' Wearie's Well.

The next step that she steppit in
She steppit to the middle;
And sighing sair says May Colvin,
" I've wat my gowden girdle."

" Wide in, wide in, thou fair May Colvin,
For ye get but scath to dwell;
O mony's the time I've watered my steeds
Wi' the water of Wearie's Well."

The neist step that she steppit in,
She steppit to the chin;
And sighing says she, May Colvin,
" This will gar twa loves twine."

" Seven king's daughters I've drowned there,
In the water o' Wearie's Well;
And I'll make you the eight o' them
And ring the common bell."

"O sin' I am standing here, quo' she,
The dowie death to die,
Ae kiss of your comely mouth
I'm sure would comfort me."

He's louted him ower his saddle-bow
To kiss her cheek and chin;
She's twined her arms round his body
And thrown him headlong in.

"Sin' seven king's daughters ye've drowned there
In the water o' Wearie's Well;
I'll make you bridegroom to them a',
And ring the bell mysell.

And aye she warsled and aye she swam
Till she swam out on land;
And aye he cried on her, May Colvin,
To haud a grip o' his hand.

"O lie thou there, thou fause Sir John,
O lie thou there," quo' she;
"For ye lie not in a caulder bed
Than the bed ye made for me;
"For the bed's nae worse your body is in,
Than ye made for my body."

And she's won home to her father's gate
About the day began to sheen.
Up then spake the wily parrot,
"May Colvin, where have you been?
And what is come o' the fause Sir John,
That woo'd you sae late yestreen?"

Up then spak the pretty parrot,
In the bonny cage where it lay,
" O what have you done wi' the fause Sir John
That ye were sae blithe of yesterday?

" He woo'd you but, he woo'd you ben,
He woo'd you into the ha',
Till once he had gotten your goodwill
For to mount and gane awa'."

" O hold your tongue, my pretty parrot,
Lay not the wyte on me;
Your cage shall be o' the beaten gowd
And the spokes of ivorie."

Up then spak the king himsell,
In the chamber where he lay;
" What ails at the pretty parrot,
He prattles sae lang ere day? "

" There came a cat to my cage door,
I thought would have worried me;
And I was calling on the king's daughter
To take the cat frae me."

LORD THOMAS AND FAIR ANNIE

I T's narrow, narrow, make your bed
  And learn to lie your lane ;
For I'm gaun ower the sea, fair Annie,
A braw bride to bring hame.
Wi' her I will get gowd and gear ;
Wi' you I never gat nane.

" But wha will bake my bridal bread
Or brew my bridal ale ?
Or wha will welcome my brisk bride
That I bring ower the dale ? "

" It's I will bake your bridal bread
And brew your bridal ale,
And I will welcome your brisk bride
That ye bring ower the dale."

" But she that welcomes my brisk bride
Maun gang like maiden fair ;
She maun lace on her girdle jimp
And braid her yellow hair."

" But how can I gang maiden-like,
When maiden I am nane ?
Have I not born seven sons to thee
And am with child again ?

" The eldest of your sons, my lord,
Wi' red gold shines his weed ;
The second of your sons, my lord,
Rides on a milk-white steed :

" And the third of your sons, my lord,
He draws your ale and wine ;
And the fourth of your sons, my lord,
He serves you bread to dine ;

" And the fifth of your sons, my lord,
He can both read and write ;
And the sixth of your sons, my lord,
Can serve red wine and white ;

" And the seventh of your sons, my lord,
Sits on the nurse's knee ;
And the eighth of your sons. my lord,
He bides in my body ;
And how can I gang maiden-like
When a maid I'll never be ? "

She's tane her young son in her arms
Another in her hand ;
And she's up to the highest tower
To see him come to land.

" Come up, come up, my eldest son,
And look o'er yon sea strand,
And see your father's new-come bride
Before she come to land."

" Come down, come down, my dear mither,
Come down frae the castle wa' !
I fear, if langer ye stand there,
Ye'll let yoursell down fa'."

And she gaed down and farther down
Her love's ship for to see :
And the topmast and the mainmast
Shone like the silver free.

And she's gane down and farther down
The bride's ship to behold ;
And the topmast and the mainmast
They shone like the beaten gold.

She's tane her seven sons in her hand
I wot she didna fail !
She met Lord Thomas and his bride
As they came ower the dale.

" You're welcome to your house, Lord Thomas,
You're welcome to your land ;
You're welcome, wi' your fair lady
That you bring by the hand.

" You're welcome to your ha's, lady,
You're welcome to your bowers ;
You're welcome to your hame, lady,
For a' thing here is yours."

" I thank thee, Annie, I thank thee, Annie ;
Sae dearly as I thank thee ;
You're the likest to my sister, Annie
That I did ever see.

" There came a knight out ower the sea
And steal'd my sister away ;
The shame scoup in his company
And land where'er he gae ! "

Annie hung ae napkin at the door,
Another in the ha';
And a' to wipe the trickling tears
Sae fast as they did fa'.

And aye she served the lang tables
With white bread and with wine;
And aye she drank the wan water
To haud her colour fine.

And aye she served the lang tables
With white bread and with brown;
And aye she turned her round about
Sae fast the tears fell down.

And he's tane down the silk napkin
Hung on a siller pin;
And aye he wipes the tear trickling
A' down her cheek and chin.

And aye he turned him round about
And smiled amang his men,
Says—" Like ye best the old lady
Or her that's new came hame ? "

When day was done and night was come
And a' men bound to bed,
Lord Thomas and his new-come bride
To their chamber they were gaed.

Annie made her bed a little forbye
To hear what they would say;
" And ever alas ! " fair Annie cried,
" That I should see this day !

" Gin my seven sons were seven young rats
Running ower the castle wa',
And I were a grey cat mysell
I soon would worry them a'.

" Gin my seven sons were seven young hares
Running ower the lily lea,
And I were a grey hound mysell,
Soon worried they a' should be."

" My gown is on," said the new-come bride,
My shoes are on my feet,
And I will to fair Annie's chamber
And see what gars her greet.

" What ails ye, what ails ye, fair Annie,
That ye mak sic a moan ?
Has your wine barrel cast the girds
Or is your white bread gone ?

" O wha was't was your father, Annie,
Or wha' was't was your mither ?
And had you ony sister, Annie,
Or had you ony brither ? "

" The Earl of Wemyss was my father,
The Countess of Wemyss my mother ;
And a' the folk about the house
To me were sister and brother."

" If the Earl of Wemyss was your father,
I wot sae was he mine ;
And it shall not be for lack o' gowd
That ye your love shall tyne.

" For I hae five ships of gay red gowd
Came ower the seas wi' me,
The twain of them will take me hame
And three I'll leave wi' thee.

" I hae seven ships of white monie
That came ower the sea the day ;
Five o' them I'll leave wi' thee,
And I'll gang hame wi' tway ;
And I'll praise God for my fair body
That I gang maiden away ! "

THE KEACH IN THE CREEL

A FAIR young may went up the street
    Some white fish for to buy,
And a bonny clerk's fa'en in love wi' her
And he's followed her by and by, by ;
And he's followed her by and by.

" O where live ye, my bonny lass,
I pray thee tell to me ;
For gin the night were ever sae mirk,
I wad come and visit thee, thee ;
I wad come and visit thee."

" O my father he aye locks the door,
My mither keeps the key ;
And gin ye were ever sic a wily wight,
Ye canna win in to me, me ;
Ye canna win in to me."

But the clerk he had ae true brother
And a wily wight was he,
And he has made a lang ladder
Was thirty steps and three, three ;
Was thirty steps and three.

He has made a cleek but and a creel,
A creel but and a pin,
And he's away to the chimby-top
And he's letten the bonny clerk in, in ;
And he's letten the bonny clerk in.

The auld wife being not well asleep
Heard something that was said ;
" I'll lay my life," quo' the silly auld wife
" There's a man in our daughter's bed, bed ;
There's a man in our daughter's bed."

The auld man he gat ower the bed,
To see if the thing was true,
But she's taken the bonny clerk in her arms
And covered him ower wi' blue, blue ;
And covered him ower wi' blue.

" O where are ye gaun now, father," she says,
" And where are ye gaun sae late ?
Ye've tane me out of my evening prayers
And o' but they were sweet, sweet ;
And o' but they were sweet."

" O wae betide ye silly auld wife,
And an ill death may ye die,
She has the muckle book in her arms
And she's prayin' for you and me, me ;
And she's prayin' for you and me."

The auld wife being not well asleep
Heard something mair was said ;
" I'll lay my life," quo' the silly auld wife
" There's a man in our daughter's bed, bed ;
There's a man in our daughter's bed."

The auld wife she gat ower the bed
To see if the thing was true ;
But what the wrack took the auld wife's fit ?
For into the creel she flew, flew ;
For into the creel she flew.

The man that was at the chimby-top,
Finding the creel was fu',
He wrappit the rape round his left shouther
And fast to him he drew, drew;
And fast to him he drew.

" O help, O help, O hinny now help,
O help, O hinny now;
For him that ye aye wished me to
He's carryin' me off just now, now;
He's carryin' me off just now.

" O if the foul thief's gotten ye,
I wish he may keep his haud,
For a' the lang winter night
Ye'll never lie in your bed, bed;
Ye'll never lie in your bed.

He's towed her up, he's towed her down,
He's towed her thro' and thro',
" O God assist," quo' the silly auld wife
" For I'm just departing now, now;
For I'm just departing now."

He's towed her up, he's towed her down,
He's gan her a right down fa',
Till every rib i' the auld wife's side
Played nick-nack on the wa', wa';
Played nick-nack on the wa'.

O the blue, the bonny bonny blue
And I wish the blue may do weel,
And every auld wife that's sae jealous o' her daughter,
May she get a good keach i' the creel, creel;
May she get a good keach i' the creel.

THE KNIFE AND THE SHEATH

IT is told, it is told, all the world over,
  The broom blooms bonnie and says it is fair,
That the king's daughter gaes wi' child to her brother,
And we'll never gang down to the broom ony mair.

He's tane his sister down to her father's deer park,
The broom blooms bonny and says it is fair,
Wi' his yew tree bow and arrows fast slung at his back,
And we'll never gang down to the broom ony mair.

" O when that ye hear me gie a loud, loud cry,
The broom blooms bonnie and says it is fair,
Shoot an arrow frae thy bow and there let me lie,
And we'll never gang down to the broom ony mair.

" And when that ye see I am lying cauld and dead,
The broom blooms bonnie and says it is fair,
Then ye'll put me in a grave wi' a turf at my head,
And we'll never gang down to the broom ony mair."

Now when he heard her gie a loud, loud cry
The broom blooms bonnie and says it is fair,
His silver arrow frae his bow he suddenly let fly ;
Now they'll never gang down to the broom ony mair.

He has houkit a grave that was lang and was deep,
The broom blooms bonnie and says it is fair,
And he has buried his sister wi' her baby at her feet,
And they'll never gang down to the broom ony mair.

And when he came hame to his father's court ha',
The broom blooms bonnie and says it is fair,
There was music and minstrels and dancing 'mang them a',
But they'll never gang down to the broom ony mair.

" O Willie ! O Willie ! what makes thee in pain ? "
The broom blooms bonnie and says it is fair,
" I have lost a sheath and knife that I'll never see again,
For we'll never gang down to the broom ony mair."

" There are ships of your father's sailing on the sea,
The broom blooms bonnie and says it is fair,
That will bring as good a sheath and a knife unto thee,
And we'll never gang down to the broom ony mair."

" There are ships of my father's sailing on the sea,
The broom blooms bonnie and says it is fair,
But sic a sheath and knife they can never bring to me ;
Now we'll never gang down to the broom ony mair."

THE JOLLY BEGGAR

THERE was a jolly beggar and a begging he was boun'
And he took up his quarters into a landward town.
And we'll gang nae mair a roving sae late into the night,
And we'll gang nae mair a roving, boys, let the moon shine
ne'er sae bright.

He wad neither lie in barn nor yet wad he in byre
But in ahint the ha' door or else afore the fire.

The beggar's bed was made at e'en wi' good clean straw and hay
And in ahint the ha' door, and there the beggar lay.

Up raise the gudeman's daughter and for to bar the door
And there she saw the beggar standin' i' the floor.

He took the lassie in his arms and to the bed he ran
" O hooly, hooly wi' me, sir, ye'll waken our gudeman."

The beggar was a cunning loon and ne'er a word he spak
Until he got his turn done syne he began to crack.

" Is there ony dog into this town ? Maiden, tell me true".
" And what wad ye do wi' them, my hinny and my doo ? "

" They'll rine a' my mealpocks, and do me mickle wrang."
" O dool for the doing o't ! Are ye the puir man ? "

And she's tane up the mealpocks and flung them o'er the wa'
" The deil gae wi' the mealpocks my maidenhead and a'."

" I took ye for some gentleman, at least the laird of Brodie
O dool for the doing o't ! Are ye the puir body ? "

He took the lassie in his arms, and gied her kisses three
And four and twenty hunder marks to pay the nourice fee.

He took a horn frae his side and blew baith loud and shrill
And four and twenty belted knights came skipping ower the hill.

And he took out his little knife, loot a' his duddies fa'
And he was the brawest gentleman that was amang them a'.

The beggar was a cunning loon and he lap shoulder height
O aye for siccan quarters as I gat yesternight ! "
      And we'll gang nae mair a roving sae late into the night,
      And we'll gang nae mair a roving, boys, let the moon shine
        ne'er sae bright.

LORD DINGWALL

W^E were sisters, sisters seven,
   Bowing down, bowing down,
The fairest women under heaven,
   And aye the birks a-bowing.*

We cast keirls us amang,
Wha would to the greenwood gang,

The keirls they gaed thro' the ha'
And on the youngest they did fa',

Now she must to the greenwood gang,
To pu' the nuts in greenwood hang,

She hadna tarried an hour but ane,
When she met with a goodly young man.

He kept her there sae late and sae lang,
Frae the evening late till the morning dawn,

He gae her a cacknet o' bonny beads
And bade her keep it against her needs,

He gae to her a gay gold ring,
And bade her keep it abune a' thing,

Three lauchters of his yellow hair,
Bade her keep them for ever mair,

* The burden, consisting of the 2nd and 4th lines, is repeated in each
subsequent verse.

99

When six lang months were came and gane,
Lord Dingwall's brought this lady hame,

There were twal' and twal' wi' baken bread,
And twal' and twal' wi' gowd sae red,

And twal' and twal' wi' bouted flour,
And twal' and twal' wi' the paramour,

Sweet Willie was a widow's son,
And at her stirrup he did run,

And she was clad in the finest pall ;
But aye she let the tears down fall.

" O is your saddle set awry ?
Or ride your steed for you ower high ? "

" Are the bridle reins for you too strang ?
Or are the stirrups for you too lang ? "

" My saddle is not set awry,
Nor is my steed for me ower high,"

" But I am weary of my life
Since I maun be Lord Dingwall's wife."

" But, little boy, will ye tell me
The fashions that are in your countrie ? "

" When ye come in upon the flour,
His mother will meet you wi' a gowden chair."

" But be ye maid or be ye none,
Unto the high seat make ye boun."

" Seven king's daughters has our lord wedded,
And seven king's daughters has our lord bedded ;

" But he's cutted their breasts frae their breastbane
And sent them mourning hame again."

That lady's called her bower maiden
That waiting was into her train ;

" I'll gie to thee five thousand marks
To sleep this night wi' my lord for me."

He's blawn his horn sae sharp and shrill,
Up starts the deer on every hill.

He's blawn his horn sae lang and loud,
Up start the deer in good green wood.

His lady mother looked ower the castle wa',
She saw them riding ane and a'.

She's called upon her maids by seven,
To make his bed baith soft and even.

She's called upon her cooks by nine,
To make their dinner fair and fine.

When they came in upon the flour
His mother met her wi' a gowden chair.

But to the high seat she made her boun ;
She knew that maiden she was none.

When night was come and day was done,
And a' men into bed were gone.

Lord Dingwall and the bonny bower maid
Into a chamber they were laid.

" Now speak to me blanket and speak to me bed
And speak thou sheet a witch's web."

" And speak up my bonny brown sword that winna lie,
Is this a maiden that lies by me ? "

" It is not a maid that you hae wedded,
But it is a maid that you hae bedded."

" It is a bed maiden that lies by thee,
But not the maiden that it should be."

O wrathfully he left the bed
And wrathfully his clothes on did.

And he has tane him thro' the ha'
And on his mother he did ca'.

" I am the most unhappy man
That ever was in Christenland."

" I thought I'd a maiden meek and mild
And I hae gotten naething but a woman wi' child."

" O stay my son into this ha',
And make good cheer wi' your merry men a'.

" And I will to the secret bower,
To see how it fares wi' the paramour."

The carline she was stark and stour,
She aff the hinges dang the door.

"O is your bairn to laird or loun,
Or is it to your father's groom?"

"O we were sisters, sisters seven,
We were the fairest under heaven."

"We cast keirls us amang,
Wha would to the greenwood gang."

"I was the youngest of us a',
The harder weird did me befa'."

"For to the greenwood I maun gae
To pu' the red rose and the dae;"

"To pu' the red rose and the thyme
To deck my mother's bower and mine."

"I hadna pu'd a flower but ane,
When by there came a goodly young man;"

"Wi' high-colled hose and low-colled shoon,
And he seemed to be some king's son."

"And be I a maid or be I nae,
He kept me there till the close of day;"

"And be I a maid or be I none,
He kept me there till the day was done."

"He gae me three locks of his yellow hair,
And bade me keep them evermair;"

"He gae me a casknet o' bonny beads,
And bade me keep them against my needs."

"He gae to me a gay gold ring
And bade me keep it abune a' thing."

O she has tane her through the ha',
And on her son began to ca'.

"What did ye wi' the bonny beads
I bade you keep against your needs?"

"What did you wi' the gay gold ring
I bade you keep abune a' thing?"

"Mither dear, I winna lie;
I gae them to a gay lady."

"But I wad gie a' my ha's and towers,
I had that lady within my bowers;"

"But I wad gie my very life,
I had that lady to my wife."

"Now keep, my son, your ha's and towers,
Ye have that lady in your bowers."

"Now keep, my son, your very life,
Ye have that lady to your wife."

Now ere a month was past and gone,
That lady bare a bonny son,

It was weel written on his breastbane,
"Lord Dingwall is my father's name."

"O row my lady in satin and silk,
And wash my son in the morning milk.

IMITATIVE BALLADS

LADY ISABEL

IT was early on a May morning
 Lady Isabel combed her hair ;
But little kent she or the morn
She wad never comb it mair.

It was early on a May morning
Lady Isabel rang the keys ;
But little kent she or the morn
A fey woman she was.

Ben it came her stepmother
Fu fair in the bower floor ;
" It's tauld me the day, Isabel
Ye are your father's whore."

" O them that tauld you that, mither,
I wish they may never drink wine ;
For if I be the same woman,
My ain sell drees the pine.

" And them that tauld you that, mither,
I wish they may never drink ale ;
For if I be the same woman
My ain sell drees the dail."

" It may be very well seen, Isabel,
It may be very well seen,
He buys to you the damask gowns,
To me the dowie green."

107

" Ye are of age and I am young,
And young amo' my flowers ;
The fairer that my claithing be,
The mair honour is yours.

" I have a love ayont the sea
And far ayont the faem ;
For ilka gown my father buys me,
My ain love sends me ten."

" Come here, come here now, Lady Isabel,
And drink the wine wi' me ;
I hae twa jewels in ae coffer
And ane o' them I'll gie thee."

" Stay still, stay still, my mither dear,
Stay but a little while,
Till I gang into Marykirk,
It's but a little mile."

When she gaed on to Marykirk
And into Mary's quire
There she saw her ain mither
Sit in a gowden chair.

" O will I leave the lands, mither,
Or will I sail the sea,
Or will I drink this dowie drink
This woman's brewed for me ? "

" Ye winna leave the lands, daughter,
Nor will ye sail the sea,
But ye will drink this dowie drink
This woman's brewed for thee.

" Your bed is made in a better place
Than ever hers will stand ;
For she shall sleep in hell's water
And ye in Heaven's land ;
Between the gold and the gilly flower
That lie down at God's right hand.

" Your bed is made in a better place
Than ever hers will be ;
And ere ye're cauld into your room
Ye will be there wi' me.

" Come in, come in now, Lady Isabel,
And drink the wine wi' me ;
I hae twa bonnie girdles in ae kist,
And ane o' them I'll gie thee."

" Stay still, stay still, my mither dear,
Stay still a little wee,
Till I gang to yon garden green
My Maries a' to see."

To some she gae the brooch, the brooch,
To some she gae the ring ;
But wae betide her stepmother,
To her she gae nae thing.

" Come in, come in now, Lady Isabel,
And drink the wine wi' me ;
I hae twa bonny birds in ae cage
And ane o' them I'll gie thee."

Slowly cam she by the bower
And slowly cam she in ;
She could fu' weel of courtesie,
Says—" Begin, mither, begin."

She put it till her cheek, her cheek,
Sae did she till her chin;
Sae did she till her fause fause lips,
But never a drap gaed in.

Lady Isabel put it till her cheek,
Sae did she till her chin,
Sae did she till her good sweet lips
And the rank poison gaed in.

" O take this cup frae me, mother,
O take this cup frae me;
My bed is made in a better place
Than ever yours will be.

" My bed is in the heavens high
Between the sun and the flowers fine;
But yours is in the lowest hell
To dree torment and pine.

" My bed is made in the fair heaven
Low down between God's feet;
My bed is gold and gilly-flower
Among the angels sweet;
But yours is made in the heavy hell
Between the wind and the weet.

WEARIESWA'

THE wind wears ower the Wearieswa'
   To the right and the left hand;
The wind wears ower by the Wearieswa'
And under by the sea sand.

Every bolt in Wearieswa'
Wi' siller was it sparred;
Every gate in Wearieswa'
Wi' red gold was it barred.

Every window in Wearieswa'
It was hasped in nickal keen;
Every bower in Wearieswa'
It was set wi' rushes clean.

There wonneth a woman in the Wearieswa',
A strong spell is her upon;
He that shall kiss her mouth for love
Of his life he is fordone.

There is nae man made of a woman
As the grass grows and the corn,
But gin he have kissed that lady's mouth
Of his life he is forlorn.

Lord Robert is ridden to the Wearieswa'
Between the low ling and the heather hie;
A wind was comen out of Wearieswa'
Between the hielands and the sea.

O whatten a wind is this weary wind,
A weary wind to me?
It's neither a scart o' the mill-water,
Nor yet a wind o' the sea.

Lady Janet looked ower by a little window,
She was fain of any man;
For the lack of love that was her in
All her body was wan.

She laid her chin out ower the wa' stanes,
All her body was weak;
The tears fell over in her face wan,
Betwixen mouth and cheek.

Gin I kissed that lady on her lips
The bitter man would I be;
Gin I kissed that lady on her hands twain
'Twere pain of my body.

O gin ye should kiss my weary hands
Your ken would be fu' sair;
And gin ye should kiss my heavy mouth
Your teen wad be mickle mair.

But ye'll gae down to yon wan water-side,
Gar make a ship of ashen tree;
And ye maun sail by seven ways
Between the faem and the green sea.

The first water ye'll sail upon
Men call it Wearieswyte;
Whoso cometh to that water
He shall have little delight.

The neist water ye'll sail upon
Men call it Wearieswan ;
Whoso cometh to that water
He is nae sicker man.

The neist water ye'll sail upon
Men call it Weariesway ;
Whose cometh to that water
He were the better away.

The neist water ye'll sail upon
Men call it Wearieswoe ;
Whoso cometh to that water
He shall neither stand nor go.

The neist water ye'll sail upon
Men call it Weariesween ;
Whoso cometh to that water
Of his body he shall have teen.

The neist water ye'll sail upon
Men call it Weariesyett ;
Whoso cometh to that water
An ill wonning he shall get.

The last water ye'll sail upon
Men call it Wearieshead ;
Whoso cometh to that water
It were better for him to be dead.

And gin the sair sea scathe you not
Nor the sea-worms in the sea,
This weary weird that is me upon
Ye shall take off from me.

And gin the water win you not upon
Ye shall have good harbouring
When ye come back to Wearieswa'
About the fair birk flowering.

And ye maun be yoursell alane
And I with a' my men,
And ye maun stand low down them amang
To see if I shall you ken.

—Gin the wan water win me not upon
Between the sea-banks and the sea,
Then I'll come back for your sake, Janet—
A token I'll hae wi' me.

But how shall ye be seen, Hynd Robert,
O how shall ye be known,
Amang so mony gentlemen
That wear the gold alone?

—O where they wear the goodly bright gold
I shall wear yellow and black;
And a little green hood behind my hair
To hang down at my back.

—But how shall ye be kent, Janet,
Or how shall ye be seen,
Among so many goodly ladies
That ye maun gang between?

O where they wear a ring, Robert,
I shall wear two or three;
And a girdle with a fair white stane,
And by that ye shall ken me.

And where they wear but yellow lammer,
I shall wear siller sheen ;
And where they gang like a queen's handmaids,
I shall gang like a queen.

A kell o' gowd abune my head
And a band abune my eebree,
And in every o' them a jewel stone
My witness for to be ;

And half my kirtle of red sendal
To hang down at my knee ;
And half my kirtle of brown sendal
That shall be wrought to me.
And the shoon on my feet of yellow samite
And by that ye shall me see.

He's made him a ship o' the goodly ash
The sides thereof were wan ;
The first water he sailed upon
He was the heavier man.

A' the oars were wrought of gold
And a' the sails of red ;
The last water he sailed upon
He seemed he was but dead.

But he's won back to Wearieswa'
That was hard on a great sea ;
His hair was fu' of the wan sea-water
And he halted of his knee.

Between the sea and the sea-banks
He's let his bonny ship stand ;
His clothes were fu' of the wan rain-water
And he halted of his hand.

Oh I will draw to me a weed,
A weed baith poor and low,
And I will gang before my lady's face,
To see if she will me know.

And he has drawn to him a weed,
A weed of yellow and black;
But there was nae hood behind his hair
To hang down at his back.

The first gate that he came to
It was little for his delight;
The knappies that were that gate upon
They were hewn of siller white.

The last gate that he came by
It was little for his ease;
Before he had well won ower it,
The blood ran frae his knees.

The neist gate that he came by
His comfort was waxen cold;
Every bolt that gate within
It was carven of red gold.

And he's gane up to the high chamber,
He's found that lady there,
The red sendal on her body,
And the red gold in her hair.

And as he stood low and very low
Amang these goodly men;
He stood amang them hoodless,
There was nae man did him ken.

And she spied him weel and very weel
Gin she might his body see;
O wha is yon gangs hoodless,
For my love it mauna be.

And she sought weel and very weel
Gin she might him behold;
She was mair fain of his fair body
Than the rain is of the mould.

And a' the men that were her before
They were red and nothing wan;
And when she saw his goodly face,
She weened it was another man.

And when she looked his face upon,
It was wan and nothing red,
And a' his hair was riven wi' rain
That rained upon his head.

O ye'll take out yon hoodless man,
That hirples on the marl;
I thought it were my love, Hynd Robert,
It is but a hireman carl.

And ye'll take out yon gangrel fellow
That hirples on the clay;
I thought it was my love, Hynd Robert,
That hae been long away.

He's taen him down to yon wan water-stand,
The tears feel ower his een;
Before he was weel in his goodly ship
The wind began to ween.

He's turned his face to the fair leeland,
He was right fu' o' care;
Before he was weel upon the sea,
The water was waxen sair.

Ye'll cast me in the heavy water
That is both green and black,
And ye'll bind my feet with a twine of silk;
Pray for the storms to slack.

Ye'll cast me in the weary water
That is both green and grey,
And ye'll bind my arms upon my back;
Pray for the rains to stay.

And they've cast over his fair body
In the water that was sae white;
And they drove over before the wind
A day's space and a night.

The first wave that cam nigh the ship
It smote her in the side;
And ever alas! quo' the ae first man,
"This water is ill to bide!"

The neist wave that cam nigh the ship,
It smote her in the head;
"Haul round, haul round," quo' the eldest man,
"This water maun be our deid!"

And they spied ower the wan sea wide
To see gin ony halp might be;
And then they saw him, Hynd Robert,
That fleeted upright in the sea.

And they spied out upon the sea,
It was a weary water and wan;
And there they saw him, Hynd Robert,
That fleeted as a living man.

" O whatten a weird is this, Hynd Robert,
That is of your body,
To fleet out ower in the easterin' wind
That thraws upon the sea ? "

The wind shall blow in the wan water,
It shall never slack for me,
Till ye bring my lady to yon sea-sand,
Cast her body in the sea.

The wind shall thraw in the wild water ;
I wot it shall never bide,
Till ye bring that lady to your sea-banks,
Cast her body ower the ship's side.

They've had that lady to yon sea-banks
And ower by yon heather hie ;
They bound her hands before her face,
Cast her body in the sea.

BURD MARGARET

"O WHA will get me wheaten bread
  And wha will get me wine?
And wha will build me a gold cradle
To rock this child of mine?

"There's nane will drink of bitter wine,
Nor eat of bitter bread;
There's nane will ca' me a clean maiden
When my body is dead.

"Nae silk maun come upon my feet,
Nae gowd into my hair;
My brothers smite me on the mouth,
Where nae man shall kiss mair."

She held her hands in the wan water
Till the fingers were a' red;
Her face was like nae fair burd's face
That was her maidenhead.

She's streekit the water on her hair,
She's signed it owre her chin,
She's streekit the water on her lips
To let the draps gang in.

The tears ran through her fair sma' mouth;
The white bones small and thin
Were waxen sharper in her lang throat,
And in her wrist and chin.

" Gin my mither has wist o' this
When she was left wi' me,
I wot these arms that are waxen lean
Had ne'er gaun round a man's body.

" Gin my mither had dreamed a dream
That sic a kail should fall on me,
She had bound me between her smock and her kirtle,
And cast me ower the sea.

" She had row'd me between her smock and her kirtle,
Let me to swim or sink ;
And I had drunken o' the saut water
Instead of tears to drink.

" The bairn that is waxen me within,
It is waxen a pain to me ;
But weel lie he and ever weel
That made my bairn's body.

" The white that was in my twa brows,
I wot it is waxen red ;
But weel lie he and ever weel
That had my maidenhead.

" O weel be to the fair red roses
Stood high against my chin ;
But ill be to the good green leaves,
For they were half the sin.

" O weel be to the little bird
Sang low against my knee ;
But ill be to my fause nourice,
She had sma' reck of me.

"O weel be to the fair red roses
Stood high against my face;
But ill be to the bonny rowan,
I wish it never grace."

Burd Margaret lay in the rank water-grass
By the fairest ford in Tyne;
And between the grass and the aspen leaf,
She saw their armour shine.

Burd Margaret lay in the low bracken
That was sae green on Tyne;
And between the reed and the wan willow,
She saw the clean steel shine.

The first of them had fair Milan coats,
The second had but pikes and jacks;
The third had coats of fair scarlet,
And gold across their caps.

There were three and three wi' bits of steel,
And three and three wi' siller fine,
And three and three wi' bits of gold,
Was red as fair new wine.

"Whatten men be these that rin," she said,
"Or whatten men be these that ride?
Either ye be thieves frae the north border,
Or men that look a bride."

"Gin I be rid frae the north border
And my braw bride won south,
I'll gar her clip me round the body
And kiss me on the mouth."

"I think ye be nae knight," she said,
"Nae knight that wons about;
There was never main but a devil
That had sae long a snout.

"Gin I should kiss your mouth," she said,
"I wis I had kissed a loon;
I think ye be some clouted carter,
Albeit ye wear steel shoon."

"I am Lord Hugh of Burnieshaw,
Ye may weel ken the face o' me;
And I wad hae back the bonnie lad bairn
That I left here wi' thee."

"Gin ye be Hughie of Burnieshaw
As I trow a better may have been,
Tell me what words I said to you,
When the rowans were green."

"O first ye pu'd the green berry,
And syne ye pu'd the red;
And the first word that ever ye spak
Was to complain your maidenhead.

"O first ye pu'd the red hollin,
And syne ye pu'd the green,
And the first word ye spak to me
Ye grat fu' sair between."

"Gin ye be Hughie of Burnieshaw,
As I think weel ye'll never be,
Here have ye back your bonny lad bairn,
That sair has troubled me."

She's caught her hand to his bridle-rein,
Held up her mouth to touch his chin ;
" Ye garred me pu' the girdle straight
That the fair knave bairn was in."

" What needs ye flur and mock, Margaret ?
What needs ye scorn at me ?
Ye never gat harm of your fause brothers,
But ye gat aye the mair gude o' me."

He's put his hands to her body,
He's laid her twart his selle ;
And ye that hae gotten a bonny sitter,
Gar keep the neist yoursell.

Aye they rode weel, and aye better,
Until the moon was nigh to sheen ;
And aye the tears ran in her breast,
And aye in the gold between.

" O whether is yon a cry of carlies,
Or men that cry on me ? "
" Bide still, bide still, now, Burd Margaret,
For ye hear naething but the sea.

" O whatten is yonder noise," she said,
" That I hear cry on us behind ? "
" Haud by my sleeve now, Burd Margaret,
For ye hear naething but the wind."

Aye they rode weel, and aye better,
Until the moon was waxen weak ;
And aye she laid her face to his,
And her tears ran by his cheek.

Aye when he kissed her bonny een,
I wot they grat fu' sair ;
Aye when she laid her head to his,
I wot the tears ran through his hair.

Aye they rode slow, and aye slower,
Till the moon's time was a' done ;
Between the road and the saddle
She thought to bear a son.

There she saw her first brother
Stood back to a fair tree ;
Said " Grace go with our bonny sister
To ride in sic a companie."

Said " Grace go with our bonny sister
To wear her gown aside ;
It is not meet for a good woman
To set her girdle wide."

He's stricken the first across the neck,
Shorn clean his beard and hair ;
" Now haud ye weel, my fair brother,
Ye'se get of me nae mair."

He's cloven the second through the chin,
The third upon the knee ;
" Now haud ye weel, my three brothers,
Ye'se get nae mair of me."

They set her in a fair bride-bed,
Full glad she was the morn ;
And between the silk and the braw geld claith,
The fair knave bairn was born.

THERE GOWANS ARE GAY

THERE gowans are gay, my joy,
   There gowans are gay,
They garr'd me wake when I should sleep
The first morning in May.

About the fields as I did pass
There gowans are gay,
I chanced to meet a proper lass
The first morning in May.

Right busy was that bonny maid
There gowans are gay,
I halsed her syne to her I said,
The first morning in May.

" O mistress fair, what do you here ? "
There gowans are gay,
" Gathering the dew, what needs ye spier ? "
The first morning in May.

" The dew " quo' I, " what can that mean ? "
There gowans are gay,
Quo' she " to wash my mistress clean."
The first morning in May.

I asked farder at her syne
There gowans are gay,
Gif to my will she would incline
The first morning in May.

She said her errand was not there
There gowans are gay,
Her maidenhood on me to ware
The first morning in May.

Then like an arrow frae a bow
There gowans are gay,
She skipt away out o'er the knowe
The first morning in May.

And left me in the garth my lane
There gowans are gay,
And in my heart a twang o' pain
The first morning in May.

The little birds they sang fu' sweet
There gowans are gay,
Unto my comfort was tight meet
The first morning in May.

And thereabout I past my time
There gowans are gay,
Until it was the hour of prime
The first morning in May.

And then returned hame bidene
There gowans are gay,
Pensant what maiden that had been
The first morning in May.

LORD SCALES

Lord Randal lay in low prison,
He looked against the wa';
Gin the big wa' stanes were linen bands,
I'd win weel through them a'.

Lord Randal sat by a low lattice,
He looked against the sea;
Gin the foul bed straws were bonny ships,
I wot weel wad I be.

Lord Randal stood by a strang window
He looked against his hand;
Gin my twa wrist chains were hempen threads,
I'd win weel to the sand.

Ye'll take the rings frae my fingers,
The silk knot frae my hair;
Ye'll gie them to the bonny knight
That cries on me sae sair.

Ye'll take the gowd bands frae my back,
The covers frae my bed;
Ye'll gie them to the Lord Randal
To put beneath his head.

Hae silk into your hands, Randal,
And gowd twine to your feet:
And braw pillows about your head
To keep your lang hair sweet.

For the rain rins through the rank bedstraw,
And the wet drips in the wa' ;
And the wee red worms in this prison
Wad gar your gowd hair fa'.

I had liefer hae my ain twa hands,
And keep my body cold ;
I had liefer hae my own twa feet
Than two sic shoon of gold.

But I had liefer hae my lady's mouth
Than the silk and the siller bands ;
But I had liefer hae her sweet body
Than a' the gowd in land.

I had liefer kiss my lady dead
Than a live woman should kiss me :
I had liefer hae my lady dead
Than a fair woman's live body.

O ye'se hae twine o' gowd for hemp,
And twine o' silk for thread ;
And ye shall hae her fair body,
But no' her body dead.

She's loosed the knot upon his back,
The knot upon his throat :
She's clad him with a suit of samite.
And red silk to his coat.

She's washed him well wi' sweet waters,
Put spice into his hair ;
She's set his feet in a narrow side chamber,
Upon a sideway stair.

He's ta'en him to her, Lady Helen,
Where she sat by a bed,
The least cloth upon her body,
It was of the noble red.

The insides of her bed curtains,
The gold was gone them through;
The outsides of her bed curtains,
They were full merry and blue.

The silk side of her bed pillows,
It was of summer green;
The gold was bound in her gold hair,
That now should tell them twa between.

O came ye for my lord's land,
Or for my lord's fee;
Or came ye for my lord's hate,
Or yet for love of me?

O gin ye come like a land robber,
For soon shall ye hang;
But gin ye come like a woman's lover,
Full sweetly ye shall gang.

O it was never for no hate,
For lord's love nor for fee:
But a' the weird that is me on
It was a' for your body.

Gin ye set nae scorn by me, Randal,
To dree a weird and a pain,
It's no Lord Scales my auld husband
That shall depart us twain.

Gin this be sooth of you, Randal,
That ye have good will to play ;
It's no Lord Scales my auld husband
Shall be better of us twey.

For I hae reapers to the land,
And sailors to the sea ;
And I hae maidens to my bower
That wait by three and three ;
And it's no Lord Scales my auld husband
Shall part my will and me.

The first draw rapes upon the ship
Between the sea and the sea sand ;
The neist they lie in the lang corn,
Wi' the reaphooks to their hand ;
And between the lang beds and the wa',
It's there the maidens stand.

She's had him to her bonnie bed,
She's laid it warm and wide ;
He's clipped that lady by the middle waist,
And by the middle side.

There was neither light nor fire them by,
And they twain were set to sleep,
When she's turned her chin to the pillow side
Made her a space to weep.

He kissed her on her fair twa breasts,
And hard upon her chin ;
He's kissed her by her white halse-bane
The little salt tears fell in.

The small tears fell about her face
Between her lips and his;
From side to side of her gold hair
Her face was full sad to kiss.

Lie down, lie down now, Lady Helen,
Lie still into my hand;
I wadna gie ane o' the pillow-beres
For ten measures of land.

Lie still into my arms, Helen,
Betwixen sheet and sheet:
I wadna gie ane o' the cods of silk
For ten measures of wheat.

Lie back into mine arms, Helen,
The gold side of the bed;
I wadna gie ane o' thy kaims o' lammer
For the gold on the queen's head.

It's I lie saft the night, Randal,
With my head against your face;
But gin ye had slept in my stables,
It had been the sweeter place.

It's I lie saft the night, Randal,
But ye'll lie hard the morn;
For I hear a mouse rin by the straw,
And a bird rin by the corn.

O whatten a bird is that, Helen,
I wad fain ken what it ails?
It's an auld bird and an ill, Randal,
Gin it be no Lord Scales.—

Then in and came her auld husband,
I wot a fu' lean bird was he;
It's wake ye or sleep ye now, madame,
Ye'se gar mak room for me.

O are ye sick the night, Lord Scales,
In the head or else the side?
Or are ye fain to sleep, Lord Scales,
For the fear ye have to ride?

Randal's taen out her girdle knife,
He's stricken him amang his e'en;
It was mair for the lady's love
Than it was for his proper teen.

Out came a' her bower maidens,
In their night smocks and night vails;
It was a' for sorrow of their lady,
It was naething for Lord Scales.

Out came a' her bower maidens,
In their sma' coats green and white;
With a red rose wrought for the left breast,
And a rose wrought for the right.

Lord Scales had on a goodly coat,
It was a' bound wi' steel thickly;
Lord Randal had but a little shirt
Between the wind and his body.

The first good straik Lord Randal strak,
The red blood sprang upon his face;
It was mair for his lady's love
Than it was for her lord's grace.

The neist good straik Lord Randal strak,
The bright blood sprang upon his nails ;
It was mair for love of Lady Helen
Than pity of Lord Scales.

Lord Scales he strak a fu' straight straik,
But Randal strak a sair ;
Lord Scales had a little joy of it,
But Lady Helen had mair.

Gar set my ships into the sea
And my hooks into the corn ;
For gin I have lost a man the night,
I'll get a man the morn.

DURIESDYKE

THE rain rains sair on Duriesdyke,
    Both the winter through and the spring ;
And she that will gang to get broom thereby
She shall get an ill thing.

The rain rains sair on Duriesdyke,
Both the winter through and the summer day ;
And he that will steek his sheep thereby
He shall go sadly away.

" Between Crossmuir and Duriesdyke
The fieldhead is full green ;
The shaws are thick in the fair summer,
And three wallheads between.

" Flower of broom is a fair flower,
And heather is good to play."
O she went merry to Duriesdyke,
But she came heavy away.

" It's I have served you, Burd Maisry,
These three months through and mair ;
And the little ae kiss I gat of you,
It pains me aye and sair.

" This is the time of heather-blowing,
And that was syne in the spring ;
And the little ae leaf comes aye to red,
And the corn to harvesting."

The first kiss their two mouths had,
Sae fain she was to greet ;
The neist kiss their two mouths had,
I wot she laughed fu' sweet.

" Cover my head with a silken hood,
My feet with a yellow claith ;
For to stain my body wi' the dyke-water,
God wot I were fu' laith."

He's happit her head about wi' silk,
Her feet with a gowden claith ;
The red sendal that was of price,
He's laid between them baith.

The grass was low by Duriesdyke,
The high heather was red ;
And between the grass and the high heather,
He's tane her maidenhead.

They did not kiss in a noble house,
Nor yet in a lordly bed ;
But their mouths kissed in the high heather,
Between the green side and the red.

" I have three sailing ships, Maisry,
For red wheat and for wine ;
The main topmast is a bonny mast,
Three furlongs off to shine.

"The foremast shines like new lammer,
The mizzenmast like steel;
Gin ye wad sail wi' me Maisry,
The warst should carry ye weel.

"Gin I should sail wi' you, Lord John,
Out under the rocks red,
It's wha wad be my mither's bower-maiden
To hap saft her feet in bed?

"Gin I should sail wi' you, Lord John,
Out under the rocks white,
There's nane wad do her a very little ease
To hap her left and right."

It fell upon the midwinter,
She gat mickle scaith and blame;
She's bowed hersell by the white water
To see his ships come hame.

She's leaned hersell against the wind,
To see upon the middle tide;
The faem was fallen in the running wind,
The wind was fallen in the waves wide.

"There's nae moon by the white water,
To do me ony good the day;
And but this wind a little slacken,
They shall have a sair seaway.

"O stir not for this nied, baby,
O stir not at my side;
Ye'll have the better birth, baby
Gin ye wad a little abide."

CLERK SAUNDERS

I<small>T</small> was a sad and rainy night
    As ever rained frae town to town,
Clerk Saunders and his lady gay,
They were in the fields sae brown.

" A bed, a bed," Clerk Saunders cried,
" A bed, a bed, let me lie down ;
For I am sae weet, and sae wearie,
That I canna gae, nor ride frae town."
" A bed, a bed," his lady cried,
" A bed, a bed, ye'll ne'er get nane.

For I hae seven bauld brethren,
Bauld are they, and very rude,
And if they find ye in bower wi' me,
They winna care to spill your blood."

Ye'll tak a lang claith in your hand,
Ye'll haud it up afore your een
And ye'll tak me in your arms twa,
Ye'll carry me into your bed
That in your bower floor I ne'er gaed.

She's tane a lang claith in her hand,
She's hauden't up afore her een
That she might swear, and save her aith,
That she saw na Sandy sin yestreen.

She's tane a lang claith in her hand,
She's hauden't up afore her ee'n
That she might swear, and save her aith,
That she saw na Sandy sin yestreen.

Then in and cam her second brother—
Says, " Twa lovers are ill to twin : "
And in and cam her thirden brother—
" O brother, dear, I say the same."

Then in and cam her fourthen brother,—
" It's a sin to kill a sleeping man : "
And in and cam her fifthen brother,
" O brother, dear, I say the same."

Then in and cam her sixthen brother,—
" I wat he's ne'er be steer'd by me : "
Then in and cam her seventhen brother,—
" I bear the hand that sall gar him dee."

Then out he drew a nut-brown sword,
I wat he stript it to the stroe,
And thro and thro Clerk Saunders' body,
I wat he garr'd cauld iron go.

Then they lay there in ithers arms
Until the day began to daw ;
Then kindly to him she did say—
" It's time, my dear, ye were awa'

" Ye are the sleepiest young man, she said,
That ever my twa een did see,
Ye've lain a' night into my arms,
I'm sure it is a shame to be."

She turned the blankets to the foot,
And turned the sheet unto the wa'
And there she saw his bloody wound,

*　　*　　*　　*　　*

O wae be to my seventhen brother !
I wat an ill death mot he dee,
He's killed Clerk Saunders, an earl's son,
I wat he's kill'd him unto me."

Then in and cam her father dear,
Cannie cam he steppin' in,—
Says, " Haud your tongue, my dochter dear,
What need you mak sic heavy meane.

" We'll carry Clerk Saunders to his grave,
And syne come back and comfort thee : "—
" O comfort well your seven sons, father,
For man sall never comfort me ;
Ye'll marrie me wi' the Queen o' Heaven,
For man sall never enjoy me ! "

EARL ROBERT

O SOME ride east and some ride north,
    And some ride west and south ;
But the ae best gate that ever I rade
Was a' for her red mouth.

O some wear blue and bonny scarlet,
And some wear green and red ;
And it's a' for love of her yellow hair
I'll wear but golden thread.

Gin this be Annie of Waterswa'
That gars ye speak sae hie,
There's nae man of your name Earl Robert,
Shall get her fair body.

O when he came by Waterswa',
The rain was sair and strang ;
Fair Annie sat in a bower-window,
And her gold hair was grown lang.

Gin I might swim to ye, Robert,
I wad never spare for gloves or gown ;
I wad never spare for the cold water,
But I have sore fear to drown.

Now God thee hold, thou fair Annie,
The wa's are hard to leap ;
The water is ill to swim, Annie,
And the brigg is ill to keep.

Gin I should open to ye, Robert,
I wis it were open shame ;
It were great pity of me, Robert,
For I gang but sick and lame.

O twice I cuttit the silk string through
That was upon my back ;
And twice I cuttit the gown away
That wadna' haud me slack.

It's ill wi' me the night, Robert,
It's weel wi' my leman ;
For the wine that comes in my fingers,
I spill it on my han' ;
And the meat that's in my very mouth,
I wot it feeds a man.

Gin I may win to ye, Annie,
The tane of us should weel fare.
There's three men keep the ways, Robert,
Between the gate and the water-stair.

I wot the night there's deep water,
Runs red upon the brim ;
It's full between the wa's, Annie,
This were but ill to swim.

There's rain the night in Carrilees,
I wot the rain is rank ;
There be twa fathoms of strang water
Between it bank and bank.

But he's rid out through Carrilees' brow,
I wot, baith wet and wan ;
Annie lay in her chamber-window,
She was a glad woman.

Between the gate and the water-stair
He made him room to stand ;
The wet ran frae his knees and feet,
It ran upon his hand.

And he's won through to her chamber,
He's kissed her neist the chin :
" O gin ye'll keep me out, Annie,
Is there ony will take me in ? "

Up then gat her auld father,
Between the wall and her bed feet ;
" Is there ony breath in your lips, Earl Robert,
To gar a dead mouth smell sweet ? "

He's tane her by the gold girdle,
He's garr'd it break atwain ;
There's nae room here for Earl Robert,
The ways are sae fou' o' rain.

He's tane a keen sword in his hand,
He's set him to the wa' ;
And the very heart's blood of Earl Robert,
I wot he's garr'd it fa'.

Out then spake she, fair Annie,
At the bed's foot where she lay ;
" There's a time for you the night, father,
And a time for us the day.

" O gin ye dig na deep, father,
I wot ye maun dig wide ;
And set my lord to the nether land,
And my bairn to the green side.

" Ye'll set my head to his foot, father,
That he be neist the sun ;
For a' that was between us twa,
I think it's a' weel done."

THE TYNESIDE WIDOW

THERE's mony a man loves land and life,
   Love's life and land and fee ;
And mony a man loves fair women,
But never a man loves me, my love,
But never a man loves me.

O weel and weel for a' lovers,
I wot weel may they be ;
And weel and weel for a' fair maidens,
But aye mair woe for me, my love,
But aye mair woe for me.

O weel be wi' you, ye sma' flowers,
Ye flowers and every tree ;
And weel be wi' you, a' birdies,
But teen and tears wi' me, my love,
But teen and tears wi' me.

O weel be yours, my three brethren,
And ever weel be ye ;
Wi' deeds for doing and loves for wooing,
But never a love for me, my love,
But never a love for me.

And weel be yours, my seven sisters,
And good love-days to see,
And long life-days and true lovers,
But never a day for me, my love,
But never a day for me.

Good times wi' you, ye bauld riders,
By the hieland and the lee ;
And by the leeland and by the hieland
It's weary times wi' me, my love,
It's weary times wi' me.

Good days wi' you, ye good sailors,
Sail in and out the sea ;
And by the beaches and by the reaches
It's heavy days wi' me, my love,
It's heavy days wi' me.

I had his kiss upon my mouth,
His bairn upon my knee ;
I would my body and soul were twain,
And the bairn and the kiss wi' me, my love,
And the bairn and the kiss wi' me.

The bairn down in the mools, my dear,
O saft and saft lies she ;
I would the mools were ower my head,
And the young bairn fast wi' me, my love,
And the young bairn fast wi' me.

The father under the faem, my dear,
O sound and sound sleeps he ;
I would the faem were ower my face,
And the father lay by me, my love,
And the father lay by me.

I would the faem were ower my face,
Or the mools on my ee-bree ;
And waking-time with a' lovers,
But sleeping-time wi' me, my love,
But sleeping-time wi' me.

I would the mools were meat in my mouth,
The saut faem in my ee ;
And the land-worm and the water-worm,
To feed fu' sweet on me, my love,
To feed fu' sweet on me.

My life is sealed with a seal of love,
And locked with love for a key ;
And I lie wrang and I wake lang,
But ye tak' nae thought for me, my love,
But ye tak' nae thought for me.

We were weel fain of love, my dear,
O fain and fain were we ;
It was weel with a' the weary world,
But O, sae weel wi' me, my love,
But O, sae weel wi' me.

We were nane ower mony to sleep, my dear,
I wot we were but three ;
But never a bed in the weary world
For my bairn and my dear and me, my love,
For my bairn and my dear and me.

THE EARL OF MAR'S DAUGHTER

IT was intill a goodly time,
  The first morning in May,
The bonny Earl of Mar's daughter
Went forth hersell to play.

She's tane her to the bonny birkenshaw
Amang the fair green leaves ;
There she saw a bonny doo
Sat on the leaf o' the tree.

" O Coo-me-doo, my love sae true,
Gin ye'll come down to me,
I'll gie ye a cage of good red gowd
For a cage of green shaw tree."

" Gowden hingers roun' your cage,
And siller roun' your wa',
I'll gar ye shine as bonny a bird
As the bonniest ower them a'."

She hadna weel these words spoken,
Nor yet she hadna said,
Till Coo-me-doo flew frae the leaves
And lighted on her head.

And she's tane hame this bonny bird,
Brought him to bower and ha' ;
She's garred him shine the bonniest bird
That was out ower them a'

When day was gane and night was come
In ae chamber they were that tide ;
And there she saw a goodly young man
Stood straight up at her side.

" How cam ye in my bower-chamber,
For sair it marvels me,
For the bolts are made o' the good red gowd
And the door-shafts of a good tree."

" O haud your tongue now, May Janet,
And of your talking let me be ;
Mind ye not on your turtle-doo
That ye brought hame wi' ye ? "

" O whatten a man are ye," she said,
" Fu' sair this marvels me ;
I doubt ye are some keen warlock
That wons out ower the sea."

" O come ye here for ills ? " she says,
" Or come ye for my good ?
I doubt ye are some strong warlock
That wons out ower the flood."

" My mither is lady of strange landis
Stand far out ower the sea ;
She witched me to a birdie's shape
For the love of your body."

" My mither is queen of the witch-landis
Lie baith to north and south ;
She witched me to a birdie's body
For the love of your goodly mouth."

" She can well of witches' work,
She maketh baith mirth and meen;
She witched me to a little bird's body
For the love of your twa grey een."

" It was a' for your yellow hair
That I cam ower the sea;
And it was a' for your bonny mouth
I took sic weird on me."

" O Coo-me-doo, my love sae true,
Nae mair frae me ye'se gae.
The stanes shall fleet on the wan waters
Before we twain be twey."

" O Coo-me-doo, my love sae true,
It's time we were abed."
" O weel for you, my ain sweet thing,
It's be as ye have said."

Then he's dwelt in her bower-chamber
Fu' six lang years and ane,
And seven fair sons she's borne to him.
Fairer was there never nane.

The first bairn she's borne to him
He's tane him ower the sea;
He's gien it to his auld mither,
Bade well-nourished it should be.

The seventh bairn she's borne to him,
He's tane him frae his make;
He's gien it to his auld mither,
Bade nourice it for his sake.

And he's dwelt in her bower-chamber
Fu' six years thro' and three ;
Till there is comen an auld grey knight
Her wed-lord for to be ;
She had nae will to his gowden gifts
Nor wad she to his fee.

Out then spak the bonny bird,
He heard what they did say ;
Says ; " Waes be to you, ye auld grey man,
For it's time I were away."

Then Coo-me-doo took flight and flew
He flew out ower the sea ;
He's lighted by his mither's castle-ha'
On a tower of gold fu' hie.

THE WORM OF SPINDLESTONHEUGH

LADY Helen sat in Spindlestonheugh
   With gold across her hair;
For every plait was on her head,
  I wot a gold piece was there.

Lady Helen sat in Spindlestonheugh
   With gold across her head;
The green gown on her fair body
   Was woven with gold thread.

Lady Helen sat in Spindlestonheugh
   Wi' silk below her breast;
The best pearl in the queen's girdle
   Was lesser than her least.

Lady Helen sat in Spindlestonheugh
   With silk upon her feet;
The seams were sewn wi' cloth of scarlet
   To keep them frae the weet.

O wha will keep the keys for me
   Until the lord be hame?
Or wha will ca' his kye for me,
   To see gin ony be lame?"

She hadna bided a month but three
   With silk bands to her side,
When word is come to Lady Helen
   To meet her father's ae new bride.

" Ye'll bring the owsen and the sheep to stall,
Ye'll bring the kye to stand ;
Ye'll set the first key in my girdle,
The neist key at my hand."

" But gin he has wedded a witch woman
To work sic teen on me,
I'll come nae mair to Spindlestonheugh
Till green grow in a dry tree.

And she's done on her braw girdle,
Between the sun and moon,
And she's done on her kaims of gold,
Her gold gown and her shoon.

She's tied her hair in three witch knots,
I wot, abune her bonny een ;
And for her hair and her body,
 I wot she might have been a queen.

" I wish the sickle was in the rye,
And the rye was ower my head ;
And aye the next rose I shall gather,
I wish the white may be the red."

She's tane the keys intil her hands
Between the red sun and the moon ;
The rain ran down upon the grass,
And stained in her silk shoon.

She's tane the keys to her girdle-tie
Between the warm sun and the weet ;
The rain that was between the grass and rye,
Ran down upon her feet.

" O whatten a burd is yonder burd
That shines about her head ? "
" It is but Helen my ae daughter
Has clad hersell wi' red,"

" O where gat she thae stones of price,
The warst might serve a queen ? "
" It is but for the summer season
She's clad hersell wi'green,"

Lady Helen knelt upon her knees,
She knelt upon her yellow hair ;
" Hae back your keys, my dear father,
God give you weel to fare."

Lady Helen knelt into the dust,
She knelt upon the roadway stane ;
" And God you keep, madame, my mither,
As I shall be your ain."

Out then spak the new-come bride,
I wot she spak wi' pain and care ;
" O some hae gold to weave, Helen,
And some hae gold to wear."

Out then spak the witch-mother,
I wot she spak fu' little worth ;
" Look where my saddle sits, Helen,
Ye'll stand against the saddle-girth."

She's tane the red kaims frae her hair,
The red shoon frae her feet ;
She's set her face to the saddle stirrup,
That nane should hear her greet.

And aye she ran, and weel she ran
Till her sides were waxen sair ;
And the sun that was upon the ways
Had burnt her through her hair.

They hadna ridden a mile but three
When she was fain to bide ;
For the blood was come upon her feet
And the pain upon her side.

And whiles she ran, and whiles she grat,
In the warm sun and the cold,
Till they came to the bonny castle
Was bigged upon with gold.

" O see ye not thae towers, Helen,
Where ye gat meat and wine ?
It's I maun ligg in the braw bride-chamber,
And ye maun ligg wi' swine.

" O see ye not thae halls, Helen,
Where ye gat silk to wear ?
It's I shall hae the gold gowns on,
When your body is bare."

" O ye'll sit in the braw guest-chamber,
And ye'll drink white and red ;
But ye'll gar them gie me the washing water,
The meats and the broken bread ? "

Ye'll get nae chine o' the broken loaves,
The white bread wi' the brown ;
Ye'll drink of the rain and the puddle water
My maids shall cast ye down."

" O ye'll sit in the braw guest-chamber
Wi' the gowd braids on your hair ;
But ye'll gie me a poor coat and a smock
For my body to wear ?

" O I shall ligg i' the trodden straw,
And ye in a gold bride-bed ;
But ye'll gie me a claith to hap my feet,
And a claith to hap my head ? "

" Ye'll get no claith to hap you in,
Ye'll get no coats of me ;
Ye'll get nae mair but a riven smock
To wear on your body."

And she's ate of the foul swines meat
With her saft lips and fine ;
She's put her mouth to the rank water,
Was poured amang the swine.

Never ae word spak Lady Helen,
Never ae word but twa ;
" O gin my mither had hands to help
I wad be weel holpen awa'."

Never ae word spak Lady Helen,
Never ae word but three :
" O gin my mither had lips to kiss,
Sae weel she wad kiss me !

" She wad kiss me on my ravelled hair,
The foul cheek and the chin ;
She wad kiss me on the weary mouth,
Where the rank water gaed in."

Out then came the witch mother :
" What ails ye now to greet ?
Here's grass to hap ye dry, Helen,
And straw to hap ye sweet."

The rain fell frae her feet and hands,
Frae her lang hair and fine :
" What ails ye at the baked meats, Helen,
The brown wheat bread and the wine ? "

She's turned her by the waist about,
She's turned her by the knee ;
She's witched her body to a laidley worm,
A laidley worm to be.

" The red fruit shall grow in green river water,
The green grass in the wet sea,
Ere ye shall come to a fair woman,
A fair woman to be."

And she's garr'd bigg her seven swine-brows,
She's made them wide and lang ;
She's tane the kail and the meal pocks
That the foul worm might feed amang.

Aye she roupit and aye she croupit
And aye she soupit the mair ;
And for the breath of her laidley mouth
The sweet land stank fu' sair.

Word is come to Lady Helen's brother,
In God's town where he lay,
His father had gatten a braw new bride
And his sister was stown away.

Word is come to Lord Richard,
Where he was in God's land,
There were nine men out of the north
Would fain be to his hand.

" Whatten word is this, ye good sailors,
This word ye hae to me ?
Gin it be a word of the good land,
A dear word it maun be."

" O there is a worm in Spindlestonheugh,
A laidley worm to see ;
It has the tongue of a maid-woman,
And a worm's foul body.

" For nine mile out of Spindlestonheugh
Of grass and rye there is nae routh ;
There is sma' routh of the good red corn,
For the breath of her rank mouth."

" Whatten word is this, ye carlish caitives ?
For this word ye hae to me,
There shall never meat come in my mouth
Till I be put to sea."

And he's garr'd bigg him a fu' fair ship,
He's biggit it a' of the rowan tree ;
It was neither hasped wi' gowd nor airn,
To haud it frae the sea.

It was neither hasped wi' gowd nor airn,
Nor yet wi' siller wan ;
But a' the wood it was biggit wi'
Was of the white rowan.

And they sailed lang, and they sailed sair
And they drave ower to South ;
And a wind was in the ship's side,
And a wind in the ship's mouth.

And when he came to Spindlestonheugh,
He's tane the vervein in his hand ;
" Now God have heed of the fair ship,
For we must row to land."

" Have pity of us, O Lord Richard,
For we dare no further gang."
" Gin I may come by a goodly gallows,
The best of ye a' shall hang."

But when he saw the seven swine trows,
He weened a sair thing to have seen ;
And when he saw the laidley worm
The tears brast ower in his een.

O' gin ye'll kiss my laidley mouth
For the love of God's body,
I winna do ye scaith, brother,
Though I be a foul thing to see."

He's put his mouth to her laidley mouth,
He's kissed her once and twice ;
" I had liever lose God's dear body
Than kiss this foul worm thrice."

He's put his mouth to her laidley mouth,
He's kissed her kisses three ;
The flesh fell frae her laidley mouth
And frae her rank body ;
And it was but his sister Helen
Stood at Lord Richard's knee.

She was clad all in fair red samite,
Her mouth was red and fair ;
There was nae burd in the good land
That had such yellow hair.

He's tane him to the witch mother
That sat by her bairn's bed ;
The gold was gone in her grey hair,
Her face was heavy and red.

" O wae be wi' you, ye ill woman,
And the young bairn at your knee ;
There's never a bairn shall die abed
That comes of your body."

" Now God you save, my fair brother,
For his dear body that was dead ;
Now God you save and maiden Mary
That kept me of her maidenhead.

WESTLAND WELL

Y E maun mak' me a scarlet gown, Lord John,
  A scarlet gown to the knee ;
It maun be sewn wi' a gowd needle,
To mak' fit wear to me.

It maun be sewn wi' a gowd needle,
And spun o' silk for thread ;
And ye maun gie me a band of silk,
To tie upon my head.
And ye maun gie me a sheet of silk
To put into my bed.

O wha was't made ye proud, Janet,
Or ever ye were born ?
There's nae gowd in the land, Janet,
Is redder than the corn.

O wha was't taught you words, Janet,
Or wha was't learned you pride ?
There's mony a better face than yours
Would fain lie neist my side.

O haud your tongue, Lord John o' the Mains,
I doubt ye hae drunken wine ;
There is not a maid that wons in heaven
Wi' sic a face as mine.

Gin I were set in the high heaven,
And God's mother were set below,
I wad be queen of the high heaven,
And she wad be let go.

When she cam in Lord John's bower,
She never had kissed man ;
When she cam frae Lord John's bower,
She was but his leman.

O ye'll gar make me a bonny bed,
Ye'll make it warm and sweet,
Ye'll set a pillow to my head, mither,
And a pillow to my feet.

It fell about the middle May time
When the apple flowers wax red,
Her mither began to chide with her
She kept sae lang abed.

I canna stand to walk, mither,
But I'm just like to die,
And wae be to your bonny bloodhound
That bit me by the knee.

Yestreen my maids took off the sheet
To wash i' the Westland Well,
And lest the bonny web suld ravel,
I set a hand mysell.

We washed the blue thread and the brown,
The white thread and the black ;
And sae cam ben your fause bloodhound,
And bit me in the back.

Sae sair it rent and bit, mither,
Sae sair it bit and clang,
And ever I hope in God, mither,
Ye'll gar that bloodhound hang.

What's this o't now maiden Janet?
What's this o't now? quo' she;
There's nae such hound that bites women,
There's nae such langs to me.

Tell me now, Janet, she says,
And I winna gar ye lee,
Is this a hound's tooth or a child's shaping
That mars your straight body?

O where your cheek was red, Janet,
Your cheek is sick and wan;
And where your back was right and flat,
It bows like a loaden man.

O where your throat was round, Janet,
It's lean and loose by this;
And where your lip was sweet, Janet,
It's grown too thin to kiss.

The blood sprang in her cheek, fair Janet,
The blood sprang in her chin;
I doubt there's ane wad kiss me, mither,
Though I be sick and thin.

About the time of moon rising
They set her saft in bed,
About the time of star setting
They streekit her for dead.

O ill be in your meat, Lord John,
And ill be in your wine;
Gin the bairn be none of your getting,
I'm sure it's none of mine.

Ill be in your bed, Lord John,
And ill be in your way,
Gin ye had been hangit a year agone,
I had been the merrier May.

LADY MAISIE'S BAIRN

"GIN ye winna cease for the pity of him,
O cease for the pity of me;
There was never bairn born of a woman
Between the sea-wind and the sea,
There was never bairn born of a woman,
That was born so bitterly."

The ship strove hard upon the wind,
I wot it drove full mightily:
But the fair gold sides upon the ship
They were bursten with the sea.

"O I am sae fain for you, Lord John,
Gin ye be no sae fain;
How shall I bear wi' my body,
It is sae full of pain?"

"O I am sae fain of your body,
Ye are no sae fain of me;"
But the sails are riven wi' the wind
And the sides are full of sea.

O when she saw the sails riven,
The sair pain bowed her back;
But when she saw the sides bursten,
I wot her very heart brak.

165

The wind waxed in the sea between,
The rain waxed in the land ;
Lord John was happed wi' saut sea-foam,
Lady Maisie wi' sea-sand ;
And the little bairn between the twa
That was to her right hand.

The rain rains saer on Duriesdyke
To the land side and the sea ;
There was never bairn born of a woman
That was born mair bitterly.

THE WITCH MOTHER

"O WHERE will ye gang to and where will ye sleep,
   Against the night begins ? "
" My bed is made wi' cauld sorrows,
My sheets are lined wi' sins.

" And a sair grief sitting at my foot,
And a sair grief at my head ;
And dule to lay me my laigh pillows,
And teen till I be dead.

" And the rain is sair upon my face,
And sair upon my hair ;
And the wind upon my weary mouth,
That never may man kiss mair.

" And the snow upon my heavy lips,
That never shall drink nor eat ;
And shame to cledding and woe to wedding,
And pain to drink and meat.

" But woe be to my bairn's father,
And ever ill fare he :
He has tane a braw bride hame to him,
Cast out my bairns and me."

" And what shall they have to their marriage meat
This day they twain are wed ? "
" Meat of strong crying, salt of sad sighing,
And God restore the dead.

" And what shall they have to their wedding wine
This day they twain are wed ? "
" Wine of weeping, and draughts of sleeping,
And God raise up the dead."

She's tane her to the wild woodside,
Between the flood and fell :
She's sought a rede against her need
Of the fiend that bides in hell.

She's tane her to the wan burnside,
She's wrought wi' sang and spell :
She's plighted her soul for doom and dole
To the fiend that bides in hell.

She's set her young son to her breast,
Her auld son to her knee :
Says, " weel for you the night, bairnies,
And weel the morn for me."

She looked fu' lang in their een, sighing,
And sair and sair grat she :
She has slain her young son at her breast,
Her auld son at her knee.

She's sodden their flesh wi' saft water,
She's mixed their blood with wine :
She's tane her to the braw-bride house,
Where a' were boun' to dine.

She poured the red wine in his cup,
And his een grew fain to greet :
She set the baked meats at his hand,
And bade him drink and eat.

Says, " Eat your fill of your flesh, my lord,
And drink your fill of your wine ;
For a' thing's yours and only yours
That has been yours and mine."

Says, " Drink your fill of your wine, my lord,
And eat your fill of your bread :
I would they were quick in my body again,
Or I that bare them dead."

He struck her head frae her fair body,
And dead for grief he fell :
And there were twae mair sangs in heaven,
And twae mair sauls in hell.

LORD SOULIS

Lord Soulis is a keen wizard,
  A wizard mickle of lear :
Who cometh in bond of Lord Soulis,
Thereof he hath little cheer.

He has three braw castles to his hand,
That wizard mickle of age ;
The first of Estness, the last of Westness,
The middle of Hermitage.

He has three fair mays into his hand,
The least is good to see ;
The first is Annet, the second is Janet,
The third is Marjorie.

The firsten o' them has a gowden crown,
The neist has a gowden ring ;
The third has sma' gowd her about,
She has a sweeter thing.

The firsten o' them has a rose her on,
The neist has a marigold ;
The third o' them has a better flower,
The best that springeth ower wold.

The kisses that are her mouth within,
There is no man knoweth of any one ;
She is a pure maid of her body,
The best that standeth under sun.

And Eastness was a bonny castle,
It lay upon a lea ;
Red wine for Annet, and white for Janet,
And water for Marjorie.

But Hermitage is a fair castle,
The fairest of the three ;
Saft beds for Annet, silk sheets for Janet,
Nane sheets for Marjorie.

He made them a' by strong cunning,
That wizard great of hand ;
The twain to fall at his life's ending,
The third alway to stand.

He made them a' by hell's cunning,
That wizard full of ill ;
They burnt up Eastness and cast down Westness
But Hermitage standeth still.

There be twenty lords in that border,
Full twenty strong lords and three,
They have sworn an oath for Lord Soulis,
Weel wroken of him to be.

They have set a meeting at Emmethaugh
And upon the Lilienshaw,
They will be wroken of Lord Soulis,
His body to hang and draw.

They have broken bread between them a'
At Ottershawe that's ower the lea,
They wad plunder Eastness and harry Westness,
But Hermitage they let be.

They watered steeds by the wan Wellhaugh
Under the sweet leaves green;
Frae the Yethburn head to Christenbury,
To ride they were full keen.

When they were come to the Yethburn spait,
I wot their knees were wet;
When they were come to the Yethburn head,
There was no porter at the yett.

When they had won to the Bloody-bush,
I wot their sides were sair;
Before they were well upon that border
They had mickle sorrow and care.
" O gin we were at the sweet Wellhaugh,
Under the merry leaves fair ! "

Before they were well on the other side
He sat a sair east them between;
" O gin we were by the Emmetburn
Under the little leaves green,
Between the birks and the Emmet water,
We had the lesser been."

When they came on that weary border,
He sent an ill thing them amang;
" We winna ride ower to Hermitage,
The wa's they are too strang;
But we will ride to the low castles,
Though the ways be ill to gang."

Out then spak Burd Marjorie's lover,
He was a fair man of his face;
" Gin I may be wroken of Lord Soulis
I have sma' care of my place;

"Gin I may be wroken of Lord Soulis
I have sma' care of ony thing ;
Of the wine for shedding, the sheets for wedding,
The kirk for christening.

"I have sma' care of my sad body
Upon the ground to gang ;
Gin I wist where I might be wroken of him
I wad give it to him strang."

Out then spak May Janet's brother,
He was a stout knight and a keen ;
"He has sent his devils us amang
To work us trouble and teen.

"Gin I wist where I might be wroken of him,
Betwixen dark and day,
I wad give baith my soul and body
To hell to fetch away."

Out then spak Burd Annet's father,
He was a good man full of age ;
"Ye'll speir at Estness, ye'll speir at Westness,
But no at Hermitage."

They turned their horse-heads round about,
Rode low down by the sand ;
And a' the way they went upon,
The devil went at their hand.

The first castle they came to,
It stood upon a sea ;
The least worth chamber in a' that castle,
It was a' whalestooth and sandal-tree.

" O whatten a may is yonder may.
Sae fair to see upon ? "
" O yonder is my daughter Annet,
Out of my ha's was gone.

" Gin ye'll come hither to me, Annet,
God's grace of me ye'se have."
" I wadna gang out, my auld fool father,
Gin ye were graithed in your grave."

" Give me three kisses, my daughter Annet,
Before my mouth is cold."
" I winna come forth for nae man's greybeard,
Till my bairn be a sennight old."

He turned his face against the sea,
His heart break right atwain ;
" The fire of hell for your body, Annet,
Ere ye behold me again."

" Pull off the green, and the goodly green,
Put on the black, the black,
For my father is ridden to Wearyland,
I doubt he'll never win back."

They turned their horse-heads round about,
Rode high upon a hill ;
And a' the gate they gaed about
The devil them garred gang ill.

The neister castle they came to,
It was hard upon the low champaign ;
The least worth bower in a' that castle,
It was a' white siller and green stane.

" O whatten a may is yonder may
That is sae great of her body ? "
" O yonder is my sister Janet,
Was stolen by night frae me.

" Gin ye'll come hither to me, Janet,
God's love of me ye'se hae."
" I wadna gang out for nae brither,
Though ye were dead the day."

" O ye'll gang down to me, Janet,
For God's sweet mercy and mine ;
For I have sought ye the lang lands ower,
These eight months wearing nine."

" I winna gang forth for nae brither,
Though his body should be lorn ;
I winna gang forth for nae man's face,
Till Lord Soulis' bairn be born."

He turned his face against the brigg,
His heart brak right in three ;
" The sorrow of hell for you, Janet,
And the warld's sorrow for me."

" Take down the red, and the bonny red,
Set up the black, the black :
For my brother is ridden to Wearies wood,
I wot he'll never win back."

They turned their horse-heads round about,
Rode back a day and twain :
And a' the rivers they rode upon
The devil rode at their rein.

175

The third castle they came to,
It was the castle of Hermitage ;
There is nae man may brake the sides of it,
Though the stanes therein are great of age.

" O whatten a may is yonder may,
That looks like ony flower ? "
" O yon is my very love, Marjorie,
Was borne out of my bower."

The bower Lady Marjorie was in,
It had neither white cloths nor red,
There were nae rushes to the bower floors,
And nae pillows to the bed.

" O will ye come down but a very little,
For God's sake or for me ?
Or will ye kiss me a very little,
But six poor kisses and three ? "

She's leaned hersell to that window,
For sorrow she couldna stand ;
She's bound her body by that window,
With iron at her hand.

She's sworn by tree and by tree's leaf,
By aits and rye and corn,
" Gin ye hadna come the night," she says,
" I had been but dead the morn."

She's kissed him under the bower-bar
Nine goodly times and ten ;
And forth is come that keen wizard
In the middest of his men.

And forth is come that foul wizard,
God give him a curse and care !
Says " The life is one time sweet to have
And the death is three times sair."

Forth is come that strong wizard,
God give him a heavy day !
Says " ye shall have joy of your leman's body
When April cometh after May."

Between the hill and the wan water
In fields that were full sweet,
There was riding and running together,
And many a man gat red-shod feet.

Between the wa's and the Hermitage water,
In ways that were waxen red,
There was cleaving of caps and shearing of jack,
And many a good man was there dead.

They have taken that strong wizard,
To bind him by the hands :
The links of airn brast off his body
Like splints of bursten birken wands.

And they have taken that foul wizard
To bind him by the feet :
The links of airn brast off his body
As berries that are burst with heat.

They have putten fire upon his flesh,
For nae fire wad it shrink :
They have casten his body in the wan well-head,
For nae water wad it sink.

Up then gat the fiend Borolallie
Bade them give ower and let be :
" Between warld's fire and warld's water
He gat a gift of me ;
Till fire came out of wan water,
There's nane shall gar him dee."

" A rede, a rede, thou fool Borolallie,
A good rede out of hand ;
Shall we be wroken of Lord Soulis
By water or by land ?
Or shall we be wroken a great way off,
Or even whereas we stand ? "

And up it spak him, foul Borolallie,
Between the tree and the leaf o' the tree ;
" Ye maunna be wroken of Lord Soulis
By land neither by sea ;
Between red fire and wan water
Weel wroken ye shall be."

And up it spak him, foul Borolallie,
Between Lord Soulis and them a' :
" Ye maunna be wroken of Lord Soulis
Betwixen house and ha' ;
But ye maun take him to the Ninestane rigs
And take his life awa'."

They have taken him to the Ninestane rigs
His foul body to slay ;
Between the whins and the whinstanes
He had a weary way.

They have taken him to the Ninestane rigs
His foul body to spill :
Between the green broom and the yellow
He gat a bitter ill.

They had a sair cast with his foul body,
There was nae man wist what to do ;
" And O gin his body were weel sodden,
Weel sodden and suppit in broo ! "

And out it spak him, foul Borolallie,
Says " whatten a coil's this coil ?
Ye'll mak a fire on the Ninestane rigs,
For a pot thereon to boil."

And out it spak him, foul Borolallie,
Saya " whatten a din's this din ?
Ye'll boil his body within the brass,
The brass to boil him in."

They boiled his body on the Ninestane rigs
That wizard mickle of lear ;
They have sodden the bones of his body,
To be their better cheer.

They buried his bones on the Ninestane rigs
But the flesh was a' clean gane ;
There was great joy in a' that border
That Lord Soulis was well slain.

A LYKE-WAKE SONG

Fair of face, full of pride,
Sit ye down by a dead man's side.

Ye sang songs a' the day:
Sit down at night in the red worm's way.

Proud ye were a' day long:
Ye'll be but lean at evensong.

Ye had gowd kells on your hair:
Nae man kens what ye were.

Ye set scorn by the silken stuff:
Now the grave is clean enough.

Ye set scorn by the rubis ring:
Now the worm is a saft sweet thing.

Fine gold and blithe fair face,
Ye are come to a grimly place.

Gold hair and glad grey een,
Nae man kens if ye have been.

THE BRIDE'S TRAGEDY

"THE wind wears roun', the day wears doun,
   The moon is grisly grey;
There's nae man rides by the mirk muirsides,
Nor down the dark Tyne's way."
In, in, out and in,
Blaws the wind and whirls the whin.

" And winna ye watch the night wi' me,
And winna ye wake the morn?
Foul shame it were that your ae mither
Should brook her ae son's scorn."
In, in, out and in,
Blaws the wind and whirls the whin.

" O mither, I may not sleep nor stay,
My weird is ill to dree;
For a fause faint lord of the south seaboard
Wad win my bride of me."
In, in, out and in,
Blaws the wind and whirls the whin.

" The winds are strang, and the nights are lang,
And the ways are sair to ride:
And I maun gang to wreak my wrang,
And ye maun bide and bide.
In, in, out and in,
Blaws the wind and whirls the whin.

" Gin I maun bide and bide, Willie.
I wot my weird is sair :
Weel may ye get ye a light love yet,
But never a mither mair."
In, in, out and in,
Blaws the wind and whirls the whin.

" O gin the morrow be great wi' sorrow,
The wyte be yours of a' :
But though ye slay me that haud and stay me,
The weird ye will maun fa'."
In, in, out and in,
Blaws the wind and whirls the whin.

When cocks were crawing and day was dawing,
He's boun' him forth to ride :
And the ae first may he's met that day
Was fause Earl Robert's bride.
In, in, out and in,
Blaws the wind and whirls the whin.

O blithe and braw were the bride-folk a',
But sad and saft rade she ;
And sad as doom was her fause bridegroom,
But fair and fain was he.
In, in, out and in,
Blaws the wind and whirls the whin.

And winna ye bide, sae saft ye ride,
And winna ye speak wi' me ?
For mony's the word and the kindly word,
I have spoken aft wi' thee."
In, in, out and in,
Blaws the wind and whirls the whin .

My lamp was lit yestreen, Willie,
My window-gate was wide :
But ye camena nigh me till day came by me
And made me not your bride."
In, in, out and in,
Blaws the wind and whirls the whin.

He's set his hand to her bridle-rein,
He's turned her horse away :
And the cry was sair, and the wrath was mair,
And fast and fain rode they.
In, in, out and in,
Blaws the wind and whirls the whin.

But when they came by Chollerford,
I wot the ways were fell ;
For broad and brown the spate swang down,
And the lift was mirk as hell.
In, in, out and in,
Blaws the wind and whirls the whin.

" And will ye ride yon fell water,
Or will ye bide for fear ?
Nae scathe ye'll win o' your father's kin,
Though they should slay me here."
In, in, out and in,
Blaws the wind and whirls the whin.

" I had liefer ride yon fell water,
Though strange it be to ride,
Than I wad stand on the fair green strand
And thou be slain beside."
In, in, out and in,
Blaws the wind and whirls the whin.

" I had liefer swim yon wild water,
Though sair it be to bide,
Than I wad stand at a strange man's hand,
To be a strange man's bride."
In, in, out and in,
Blaws the wind and whirls the whin.

" I had liefer drink yon dark water,
Wi' the stanes to make my bed,
And the faem to hide me, and thou beside me,
Than I wad see thee dead."
In, in, out and in,
Blaws the wind and whirls the whin.

He's kissed her twice, he's kissed her thrice,
On cheek and lip and chin :
He's wound her rein to his hand again,
And lightly they leapt in.
In, in, out and in,
Blaws the wind and whirls the whin.

Their hearts were high to live or die,
Their steeds were stark of limb :
But the stream was starker, the spate was darker,
Than man might live and swim.
In, in, out and in,
Blaws the wind and whirls the whin.

The first ae step they strode therein,
It smote them foot and knee :
But ere they wan to the mid water
The spate was as the sea.
In, in, out and in,
Blaws the wind and whirls the whin.

But when they wan to the mid water,
It smote them hand and head :
And nae man knows but the wave that flows
Where they lie drowned and dead.
In, in, out and in,
Blaws the wind and whirls the whin.

MODERN BALLADS

THE BALLAD OF DEAD MEN'S BAY

THE sea swings owre the slants of sand,
    All white with winds that drive;
The sea swirls up to the still dim strand,
    Where nae man comes alive.

At the grey soft edge of the fruitless surf
    A light flame sinks and springs;
At the grey soft rim of the flowerless turf
    A low flame leaps and clings.

What light is this on a sunless shore,
    What gleam on a starless sea?
Was it earth's or hell's waste womb that bore
    Such births as should not be?

As lithe snakes turning, as bright stars burning,
    They bicker and beckon and call;
As wild waves churning, as wild winds yearning,
    They flicker and climb and fall.

A soft strange cry from the landward rings—
    "What ails the sea to shine?"
A keen sweet note from the spray's rim springs—
    "What fires are these of thine?"

A soul am I that was born on earth
    For ae day's waesome span:
Death bound me fast on the bourn of birth
    Ere I were christened man.

" A light by night, I fleet and fare
   Till the day of wrath and woe;
On the hems of earth and the skirts of air
   Winds hurl me to and fro."

" O well is thee, though the weird be strange
   That bids thee flit and flee;
For hope is child of the womb of change,
   And hope keeps watch with thee.

" When the years are gone, and the time is come,
   God's grace may give thee grace;
And thy soul may sing, though thy soul were dumb,
   And shine before God's face.

" But I, that lighten and revel and roll
   With the foam of the plunging sea,
No sign is mine of a breathing soul
   That God should pity me.

" Nor death, nor heaven, nor hell, nor birth
   Hath part in me nor mine:
Strong lords are these of the living earth
   And loveless lords of thine.

" But I that know nor lord nor life
   More sure than storm or spray,
Whose breath is made of sport and strife,
   Whereon shall I find stay?"

" And wouldst thou change thy doom with me,
   Full fain with thee would I:
For the life that lightens and lifts the sea
   Is more than earth or sky.

" And what if the day of doubt and doom
    Shall save nor smite not me ?
I would not rise from the slain world's tomb
    If there be no more sea.

" Take he my soul that gave my soul,
    And give it thee to keep ;
And me, while seas and stars shall roll
    Thy life that falls on sleep."

That word went up through the mirk mid sky,
    And even to God's own ear :
And the Lord was ware of the keen twin cry,
    And wroth was he to hear.

He's tane the soul of the unsained child
    That fled to death from birth ;
He's tane the light of the wan sea wild,
    And bid it burn on earth.

He's given the ghaist of the babe new-born
    The gift of the water-sprite,
To ride on revel from morn to morn
    And roll from night to night.

He's given the sprite of the wild wan sea
    The gift of the new-born man,
A soul for ever to bide and be
    When the years have filled their span.

When a year was gone and a year was come,
    O loud and loud cried they—
" For the lee-lang year thou hast held us dumb
    Take now thy gifts away ! "

O loud and lang they cried on him,
  And sair and sair they prayed :
" Is the face of thy grace as the night's face grim
  For those thy wrath has made ! "

A cry more bitter than tears of men
  From the rim of the dim grey sea ;—
" Give me my living soul again,
  The soul thou gavest me,
The doom and the dole of kindly men,
  To bide my weird and be ! "

A cry more keen from the wild low land
  Than the wail of waves that roll ;—
" Take back the gift of a loveless hand,
  Thy gift of doom and dole,
The weird of men that bide on land ;
  Take from me, take my soul ! "

The hands that smite are the hands that spare ;
  They build and break the tomb ;
They turn to darkness and dust and air
  The fruits of the waste earth's womb ;
But never the gift of a granted prayer,
  The dole of a spoken doom.

Winds may change at a word unheard,
  But none may change the tides :
The prayer once heard is a God's own word ;
  The doom once dealt abides.

And ever a cry goes up by day,
  And ever a wail by night ;
And nae ship comes by the weary bay
But her shipmen hear them wail and pray,
  And see with earthly sight

The twofold flames of the twin lights play
Where the sea-banks green and the sea-floods gray
Are proud of peril and fain of prey,
And the sand quakes ever; and ill fare they
    That look upon that light.

THE KING'S DAUGHTER

WE were ten maidens in the green corn,
  Small red leaves in the mill-water;
Fairer maidens never were born,
  Apples of gold for the king's daughter.

We were ten maidens by a well-head,
  Small white birds in the mill-water :
Sweeter maidens never were wed,
  Rings of red for the king's daughter.

Thr first to spin, the second to sing,
  Seeds of wheat in the mill-water ;
The third may was a goodly thing,
  White bread and brown for the king's daughter.

The fourth to sew and the fifth to play,
  Fair green weed in the mill-water ;
The sixth may was a goodly may,
  White wine and red for the king's daughter.

The seventh to woo, the eighth to wed,
  Fair thin reeds in the mill-water ;
The ninth had gold work on her head,
  Honey in the comb for the king's daughter.

The ninth had gold work round her hair,
  Fallen flowers in the mill-water ;
The tenth may was goodly and fair,
  Golden gloves for the king's daughter.

We were ten maidens in a field green,
  Fallen fruit in the mill-water ;
Fairer maidens never have been,
  Golden sleeves for the king's daughter.

By there comes the king's young son,
  A little wind in the mill-water ;
" Out of ten maidens ye'll grant me one,"
  A crown of red for the king's daughter.

" Out of ten mays ye'll give me the best,"
  A little rain in the mill-water ;
A bed of yellow straw for all the rest,
  A bed of gold for the king's daughter.

He's ta'en out the goodliest,
  Rain that rains in the mill-water ;
A comb of yellow shell for all the rest,
  A comb of gold for the king's daughter.

He's made her bed to the goodliest,
  Wind and hail in the mill-water ;
A grass girdle for all the rest,
  A girdle of arms for the king's daughter.

He's set his heart to the goodliest,
  Snow that snows in the mill-water ;
Nine little kisses for all the rest,
  An hundred fold for the king's daughter.

He's ta'en his leave at the goodliest,
  Broken boats in the Mill-water,
Golden gifts for all the rest,
  Sorrow of heart for the king's daughter.

" Ye'll make a grave for my fair body,"
  Running rain in the mill-water;
" And ye'll streek my brother at the side of me,"
  The pains of hell for the king's daughter.

THE SEA-SWALLOWS

THIS fell when Christmas lights were done,
  (Red rose leaves will never make wine)
But before the Easter lights begun;
  The ways are sair fra' the Till to the Tyne.

Two lovers sat where the rowan blows
  And all the grass is heavy and fine,
By the gathering-place of the sea-swallows
  When the wind brings them over Tyne.

Blossom of broom will never make bread,
  Red rose leaves will never make wine;
Between her brows she is grown red,
  That was full white in the fields by Tyne.

" O what is this thing ye have on,
  Show me now, sweet daughter of mine ? "
" O father, this is my little son
  That I found hid in the sides of Tyne.

" O what will ye give my son to eat,
  Red rose leaves will never make wine ? "
" Fen-water and adder's meat."
  The ways are sair fra' the Till to the Tyne.

" Or what will ye get my son to wear ? "
  (Red rose leaves will never make wine)
" A weed and a web of nettle's hair."
  The ways are sair fra' the Till to the Tyne.

" Or what will ye take to line his bed ? "
   (Red rose leaves will never make wine)
" Two black stones at the kirkwall's head."
   The ways are sair fra' the Till to the Tyne.

" Or what will ye give my son for land ? "
   (Red rose leaves will never make wine)
" Three girl's paces of red sand."
   The ways are sair fra' the Till to the Tyne.

" Or what will ye give me for my son ? "
   (Red rose leaves will never make wine)
" Six times to kiss his young mouth on."
   The ways are sair fra' the Till to the Tyne.

" But what have ye done with the bearing-bread,
   And what have ye made of the washing-wine ?
Or where have ye made your bearing-bed,
   To bear a son in the sides of Tyne ? "

" The bearing-bread is soft and new,
   There is no soil in the straining wine ;
The bed was made between green and blue,
   It stands full soft by the sides of Tyne.

" The fair grass was my bearing-bread,
   The well-water my washing wine ;
The low leaves were my bearing-bed,
   And that was best in the sides of Tyne."

" O daughter, if ye have done this thing,
   I wot the greater grief is mine ;
This was a bitter child-bearing,
   When ye were got by the sides of Tyne.

" About the time of sea-swallows
    That fly full thick by six and nine,
Ye'll have my body out of the house,
    To bury me by the sides of Tyne.

" Set nine stones by the wall for twain,"
    (Red rose leaves will never make wine)
" For the bed I take will measure ten."
    The ways are sair fra' the Till to the Tyne.

" Tread twelve girl's paces out for three,"
    (Red rose leaves will never make wine)
" For the pit I made has taken me."
    The ways are sair fra' the Till to the Tyne.

A FRAGMENT OF A BORDER BALLAD

Duke Loys is set on his bridge-way,
He held by the hand a right fair may,
" Ye'll give me a knight of little birth,
That is not well six tyrants worth."

" Oh, I will have him certainly,
Despite my mother that carried me ;
Despite friend, and brother also,
And you, my father, that I love so."

" Daughter, put this love aside,
Or in the tower ye maun bide,"
" I more liefer in the tower abide
Than I would set this love aside."

" Put in my daughter out of light,
That she shall think all days be night."
There was gone out the seventh year
When he went in to talk with her.

" Good morrow, daughter, how fare you ? "
" Ill fares it, father, to say true ;
The earth has rotten away my feet,
And the worms have gotten my sides to eat."

" Daughter, put thy love aside,
Or in the tower ye must bide."
" I had liefer in the tower abide,
Father, than set my love aside."

THE WEARY WEDDING

O DAUGHTER, why do ye laugh and weep,
   One with another ?
For woe to wake and for will to sleep,
   Mother, my mother.

But weep ye winna the day ye wed,
   One with another.
For tears are dry when the springs are dead,
   Mother, my mother.

Too long have your tears run down like rain,
   One with another.
For a long love lost and a sweet love slain,
   Mother, my mother.

Too long have your tears dripped down like dew,
   One with another.
For a knight that my sire and my brethren slew,
   Mother, my mother.

Let past things perish and dead griefs lie,
   One with another.
O fain would I weep not, and fain would I die,
   Mother, my mother.

Fair gifts we give ye, to laugh and live,
   One with another.
But sair and strange are the gifts I give,
   Mother, my mother.

And what will ye give for your father's love ?
  One with another.
Fruits full few and thorns enough,
  Mother, my mother.

And what will ye give for your mother's sake ?
  One with another.
Tears to brew and tares to bake,
  Mother, my mother.

And what will ye give your sister Jean ?
  One with another.
A bier to build and a babe to wean,
  Mother, my mother.

And what will ye give your sister Nell ?
  One with another.
The end of life and beginning of hell,
  Mother, my mother.

And what will ye give your sister Kate ?
  One with another.
Earth's door and hell's gate,
  Mother, my mother.

And what will ye give your brother Will ?
  One with another.
Life's grief and world's ill,
  Mother, my mother.

And what will ye give your brother Hugh ?
  One with another.
A bed of turf to turn into,
  Mother, my mother.

And what will ye give your brother John?
  One with another.
The dust of death to feed upon,
  Mother, my mother.

And what will ye give your bauld bridegroom?
  One with another.
A barren bed and an empty room,
  Mother, my mother.

And what will ye give your bridegroom's friend?
  One with another.
A weary foot to the weary end,
  Mother, my mother.

And what will ye give your blithe bridesmaid?
  One with another.
Grief to sew and sorrow to braid.
  Mother, my mother.

And what will ye drink the day ye're wed?
  One with another.
But ae drink of the wan well-head,
  Mother, my mother.

And whatten a water is that to draw?
  One with another.
We maun drae thereof a', we maun drink thereof a',
  Mother, my mother.

And what shall ye pu' where the well rins deep?
  One with another.
Green herb of death, fine flower of sleep,
  Mother, my mother.

Are there ony fishes that swim therein ?
    One with another.
The white fish grace, and the red fish sin,
    Mother, my mother.

Are there ony birds that sing thereby ?
    One with another.
O when they come thither they sing till they die,
    Mother, my mother.

Is there ony draw-bucket to that well-head ?
    One with another.
There's a wee well-bucket hangs low by a thread,
    Mother, my mother.

And whatten a thread is that to spin ?
    One with another.
It's green for grace, and it's black for sin,
    Mother, my mother.

And what will ye strew on your bride-chamber floor ?
    One with another.
But one strewing and no more,
    Mother, my mother.

And whatten a strewing shall that one be ?
    One with another.
The dust of earth and sand of the sea,
    Mother, my mother.

And what will ye take to build your bed ?
    One with another.
Sighing and shame and the bones of the dead,
    Mother, my mother.

And what will ye wear for your wedding gown ?
  One with another.
Grass for the green and dust for the brown,
  Mother, my mother.

And what will ye wear for your wedding lace ?
  One with another.
A heavy heart and a hidden face.
  Mother, my mother.

And what will ye wear for a wreath to your head ?
  One with another.
Ash for the white and blood for the red,
  Mother, my mother.

And what will ye wear for your wedding ring ?
  One with another.
A weary thought for a weary thing,
  Mother, my mother.

And what shall the chimes and the bell-ropes play ?
  One with another.
A weary tune on a weary day,
  Mother, my mother.

And what shall be sung for your wedding song ?
  One with another.
A weary word of a weary wrong,
  Mother, my mother.

The world's way with me runs back,
  One with another,
Wedded in white and buried in black,
  Mother, my mother.

The world's day and the world's night,
  One with another,
Wedded in black and buried in white,
  Mother, my mother.

The world's bliss and the world's teen,
  One with another,
It's red for white and it's black for green,
  Mother, my mother.

The world's will and the world's way,
  One with another,
It's sighing for night and crying for day,
  Mother, my mother.

The world's good and the world's worth,
  One with another,
It's earth to flesh and it's flesh to earth,
  Mother, my mother.

*   *   *   *   *

When she came out at the kirkyard gate,
  (One with another)
The bridegroom's mother was there in wait.
  (Mother, my mother).

O mother, where is my great green bed,
  (One with another)
Silk at the foot and gold at the head,
  Mother, my mother ?

Yea, it is ready, the silk and the gold,
  One with another,
But line it well that I lie not cold,
  Mother, my mother.

She laid her cheek to the velvet and vair,
  One with another ;
She laid her arms up under her hair,
  (Mother, my mother.)

Her gold hair fell through her arms fu' low,
  One with another,
Lord God, bring me out of woe !
  (Mother, my mother.)

Her gold hair fell in the gay reeds green,
  One with another :
Lord God, bring me out of teen !
  (Mother, my mother.)

*　　*　　*　　*　　*

O mother, where is my lady gone ?
  (One with another.)
In the bride-chamber she makes sore moan :
  (Mother, my mother.)

Her hair falls over the velvet and vair,
  (One with another)
Her great soft tears fall over her hair.
  (Mother, my mother.)

When he came into the bride's chamber,
  (One with another)
Her hands were like pale yellow amber.
  (Mother, my mother.)

Her tears made specks in the velvet and vair,
  (One with another)
The seeds of the reeds made specks in her hair.
  (Mother, my mother.)

He kissed her under the gold on her head ;
   (One with another)
The lids of her eyes were like cold lead,
   (Mother, my mother.)

He kissed her under the fall of her chin ;
   (One with another)
There was right little blood therein.
   (Mother, my mother.)

He kissed her under her shoulder sweet ;
   (One with another)
Her throat was weak, with little heat.
   (Mother, my mother.)

He kissed her down by her breast-flowers red,
   One with another ;
They were like river-flowers dead.
   (Mother, my mother.)

What ails you now o' your weeping, wife ?
   (One with another.)
It ails me sair o' my very life.
   (Mother, my mother).

What ails you now o' your weary ways ?
   (One with another.)
It ails me sair o' my long life-days.
   (Mother, my mother.)

Nay, ye are young, ye are over fair.
   (One with another.)
Though I be young, what needs ye care ?
   (Mother, my mother.)

Nay, ye are fair, ye are over sweet.
   (One with another.)
Though I be fair, what needs ye greet?
   (Mother, my mother.)

Nay, ye are mine while I hold my life.
   (One with another.)
O fool, will ye marry the worm for a wife?
   (Mother, my mother.)

Nay, ye are mine while I have my breath.
   (One with another.)
O fool, will ye marry the dust of death?
   (Mother, my mother.)

Yea, ye are mine, we are handfast wed,
   One with another.
Nay, I am no man's ; nay, I am dead,
   Mother, my mother.

A REIVER'S NECK-VERSE

SOME die singing, and some die swinging,
And weel mot a' they be :
Some die playing, and some die praying,
And I wot say winna we, my dear,
And I wot sae winna we.

Some die sailing, and some die wailing,
And some die fair and free :
Some die flyting, and some die fighting,
But I for a fause love's fee, my dear,
But I for a fausse love's fee.

Some die laughing, and some die quaffing,
And some die high on tree :
Some die spinning, and some die sinning,
But faggot and fire for ye, my dear,
Faggot and fire for ye.

Some die weeping, and some die sleeping,
And some die under sea :
Some die ganging, and some die hanging,
And a twine of a tow for me, my dear,
And a twine of a tow for me.

THE KING'S AE SON

Quo' the bracken-bush to the wan well-head,
"O whatten a man is this man dead?"

"O this is the King's ae son," quo' she,
"That lies here dead upon my knee."

"What will ye do wi' the King's ae son?"
"The little fishes shall feed him on."

"What will ye strew for his body's bed?"
"Green stanes aneath his head."

"What will ye gie for his body's grace?"
"Green leaves abune his face."

"What will ye do wi' the rings on his hand?"
"Hide them ower wi' stane and sand."

"What will ye do wi' the gowd in his hair?"
"Hide it ower wi' rushes fair."

"What will he have when the hill winds blow?"
"Cauld rain and routh of snow."

"What shall he get when the birds fly in?"
"Death for sorrow, and sorrow for sin."

"What shall come to his father, the King?"
"Long life and a heavy thing."

" What shall come to his mother, the Queen ? "
" Grey hairs and a bitter teen."

" What to his leman, that garr'd him be slain ? "
" Hell's pit and hell's pain."

MAY JANET

"STAND up, stand up, thou May Janet,
    And go to the wars with me."
He's drawn her by both hands
With her face against the sea.

" He that strews red shall gather white,
He that sews white reap red,
Before your face and my daughter's
Meet in a marriage-bed.

Gold coin shall grow in the yellow field,
Green corn in the green sea-water,
And red fruit grow of the rose's red,
Ere your fruit grow in her."

" But I shall have her by land," he said,
" Or I shall have her by sea,
Or I shall have her by strong treason
And no grace go with me."

Her father's drawn her by both hands,
He's rent her gown from her,
He's ta'en the smock round her body,
Cast in the sea-water.

The captain's drawn her by both sides
Out of the fair green sea ;
" Stand up, stand up, thou May Janet,
And come to the war with me."

The first town they came to
There was a blue bride-chamber ;
He clothed her on with silk
And belted her with amber.

The second town they came to
The bridesmen feasted knee to knee ;
He clothed her on with silver,
A stately thing to see.

The third town they came to
The bridesmaids all had gowns of gold ;
He clothed her on with purple,
A rich thing to behold.

The last town they came to
He clothed her white and red,
With a green flag either side of her
And a gold flag overhead.

A JACOBITE'S FAREWELL. (1716)

THERE's nae mair lands to tyne, my dear,
   And nae mair lives to gie :
Though a man think sair to live nae mair,
   There's but one day to die.

For a' things come and a' days gane,
   What needs ye rend your hair ?
But kiss me till the morn's morrow,
   Then I'll kiss ye nae mair.

O lands are lost and life's losing,
   And what were they to gie ?
Fu' mony a man gives all he can,
   But nae man else gives ye.

Our king wons ower the sea's water,
   And I in prison sair :
But I'll win out the morn's morrow,
   And ye'll see me nae mair.

A JACOBITE'S EXILE. (1746)

THE weary day rins down and dies,
 The weary night wears through :
And never an hour is fair wi' flower,
And never a flower wi' dew.

I would the day were night for me,
I would the night were day :
For then would I stand in my ain fair land,
As now in dreams I may.

O lordly flow the Loire and Seine,
And loud the dark Durance :
But bonnier shine the braes of Tyne
Than a' the fields of France ;
And the waves of Till that speak sae still
Gleam goodlier where they glance.

O weel were they that fell fighting
On dark Drumossie's day :
They keep their hame ayont the faem,
And we die far away.

O sound they sleep, and saft, and deep,
But night and day wake we ;
And ever between the sea-banks green
Sounds loud the sundering sea.

And ill we sleep, sae sair we weep,
But sweet and fast sleep they ;
And the mool that haps them roun' and laps them
Is e'en their country's clay ;
But the land we tread that are not dead
Is strange as night by day.

Strange as night in a strange man's sight,
Though fair as dawn it be :
For what is here that a stranger's cheer
Should yet wax blithe to see ?

The hills stand steep, the dells lie deep,
The fields are green and gold :
The hill-streams sing, and the hill-sides ring,
As ours at home of old.

But hills and flowers are nane of ours,
And ours are oversea :
And the kind strange land whereon we stand,
It wotsna what were we
Or ever we came, wi' scathe and shame,
To try what end might be.

Scathe, and shame, and a waefu' name,
And a weary time and strange,
Have they that seeing a weird for dreeing
Can die, and cannot change.

Shame and scorn may we thole that mourn,
Though sair be they to dree :
But ill may we bide the thoughts we hide,
Mair keen than wind and sea.

Ill may we thole the night's watches,
And ill the weary day ;
And the dreams that keep the gates of sleep,
A waefu' gift gie they ;
For the sangs they sing us, the sights they bring us,
The morn blows all away.

On Aikenshaw the sun blinks braw,
The burn rins blithe and fain :
There's nought wi' me I wadna gie
To look thereon again.

On Keilder-side the wind blaws wide ;
There sounds nae hunting horn
That rings sae sweet as the winds that beat
Round banks where Tyne is born.

The Wansbeck sings with all her springs,
The bents and braes give ear ;
And the wood that rings wi' the sang she sings
I may not see nor hear ;
For far and far thae blithe burns are,
And strange is a' thing near.

The light there lightens, the day there brightens,
The loud wind there lives free :
Nae light comes nigh me or wind blaws by me
That I wad hear or see.

But O gin I were there again,
Afar ayont the faem,
Cauld and dead in the sweet saft bed
That haps my sires at hame !

We'll see nae mair the sea-banks fair,
And the sweet grey gleaming sky,
And the lordly strand of Northumberland,
And the goodly towers thereby :
And none shall know but the winds that blow
The graves wherein we lie.

THE BLOODY SON

" O WHERE have ye been the morn sae late,
My merry son, come tell me hither ?
O where have ye been the morn sae late ?
And I wot I hae not anither."
" By the water-gate, by the water-gate,
O dear mither."

" And whatten kin' o' wark had ye there to make,
My merry son, come tell me hither ?
And whatten kin' o' wark had ye there to make ?
And I wot I hae not anither."
" I watered my steeds with water frae the lake,
O dear mither."

" Why is your coat sae fouled the day,
My merry son, come tell me hither ?
Why is your coat sae fouled the day ?
And I wot I hae not anither."
" The steeds were stamping sair by the weary banks of clay,
O dear mither."

" And where gat ye thae sleeves of red,
My merry son, come tell me hither ?
And where gat ye thae sleeves of red ?
And I wot I hae not anither."
" I have slain my brither by the weary waterhead,
O dear mither."

And where will ye gang to mak your mend,
My merry son, come tell me hither ?
And where will ye gang to mak your mend ?
And I wot I hae not anither."
" The warldis way, to the warldis end,
O dear mither."

" And what will ye leave your father dear,
My merry son, come tell me hither ?
And what will ye leave your father dear ?
And I wot I hae not anither."
" The wood to fell and the logs to bear,
For he'll never see my body mair,
O dear mither."

" And what will ye leave your mither dear,
My merry son, come tell me hither ?
And what will ye leave your mither dear ?
And I wot I hae not anither."
" The wool to card and the wool to wear,
For ye'll never see my body mair,
O dear mither."

" And what will ye leave for your wife to take,
My merry son, come tell me hither ?
And what will ye leave for your wife to take ?
And I wot I hae not anither."
" A goodly gown and a fair new make,
For she'll do nae mair for my body's sake,
O dear mither."

" And what will ye leave your young son fair,
My merry son, come tell me hither ?
And what will ye leave your young son fair ?
And I wot ye hae not anither."

" A twiggen school-rod for his body to bear,
Though it garred him greet he'll get nae mair,
O dear mither."

" And what will ye leave your little daughter sweet,
My merry son, come tell me hither ?
And what will ye leave your little daughter sweet ?
And I wot ye hae not anither."
" Wild mulberries for her mouth to eat,
She'll get nae mair though it garred her greet,
O dear mither."

" And when will ye come back frae roamin',
My merry son, come tell me hither ?
And when will ye come back frae roamin' ?
And I wot I hae not anither."
" When the sunrise out of the north is comen,
O dear mither."

" When shall the sunrise on the north side be,
My merry son, come tell me hither ?
When shall the sunrise on the north side be ?
And I wot I hae not anither."
" When chuckie-stanes shall swim in the sea,
O dear mither."

" When shall stanes in the sea swim,
My merry son, come tell me hither."
When shall stanes in the sea swim ?
And I wot I hae not anither."
" When birdies' feathers are as lead therein,
O dear mither."

" When shall feathers be as lead,
My merry son, come tell me hither ?
When shall feathers be as lead ?
And I wot I hae not anither."
" When God shall judge between the quick and the dead,
O dear mither."

" O whatten a wreck wad they seek on land,"
   (Sweet fruits are sair to gather)
" That they houk the turf to the seaward hand ? "
   And the wind wears owre the heather.

" O whatten a prey wad they think to take "
   (Sweet fruits are sair to gather)
" That they delve the dykes for a dead man's sake ? "
   And the wind wears owre the heather.

A bane of the dead in his hand he's tane ;
   Sweet fruits are sair to gather :
And the red blood brak frae the dead white bane.
   And the wind wears owre the heather.

He's cast it forth of his auld faint hand ;
   Sweet fruits are sair to gather :
And the red blood ran on the wan wet sand.
   And the wind wears owre the heather.

" O whatten a slayer is this," they said,
   (Sweet fruits are sair to gather)
" That the straik of his hand should raise his dead ? "
   And the wind wears owre the heather.

" O weel is me for the sign I take,"
   (Sweet fruits are sair to gather)
" That now I may die for my auld sin's sake,"
   And the wind wears owre the heather.

" For the dead was in wait now fifty year,"
   (Sweet fruits are sair to gather)
" And now shall I die for his blood's sake here,"
   And the wind wears owre the heather.

BORDER BALLAD

THE leaves are green in the good summer,
  The grass is green and long,
Frae the Ailsenshaw to the wat Wellhaugh
The sun was set and strong.

O the Earl's seat is wat wi' dew,
And the way is hard to see ;
She's ca'd to her her bower-maidens,
She's ca'd them a' but three.

The tane o' thae was her girdle-maid,
The tane looked ower the wa',
The third sat in the south chamber,
And that was warst of a'.

When they came ower by O Hershaw
They were twenty men to see ;
When they came back frae the Ailsenshaw,
They were but ane and three.

" Often have I gane this way
Ayont the Earl's seat ;
But now I maun gang this way
Wi' fetters on my feet.

Often have I gane this way
Wi' twenty men and three,
But ever the best of a' my men
Are dead for love o' me."

had been mixed up with it. In all the later editions of the
" Minstrelsy " it appears deluged and stifled with modern rubbish
of the basest counterfeit fashion, but still retaining a human
form. Later editors, feeling that all was not yet done as long as
the best verses were spared, have seized, mutilated and turned it
out upon the world with no shape left it. The two other versions extant (both given at full in the valuable and careful
appendix to Mr. Child's first volume, where those who can
may look up the various readings which I have here no space
for), are decayed and enfeebled by age alone, having suffered no
wilful violence at the hands of their writers. I have gathered
some few good verses from them, all that appeared to fit well into
the genuine text; by their help have here and there recovered
the true reading in place of a futile or defective passage. Scott's
first text has been my chief guide as may be seen on reference to
the " Ministrelsy " of 1803.

Cancelled in the Manuscript.

I may give in this place two stanzas which perhaps should not
have been rejected, but that there seemed no absolute need of
them : one following the line " For nae lord that ye hae ; "

> Then out it speaks her brither dear,
> He meant to do her harm ;
> There is a herb in Carterhaugh
> Will twine you and the bairn.

(Should not the word " gravil " a little further on be " savin,"
which was often used to procure abortions ? I did not wish to
throw out " gravil " without absolute reason, but have little
doubt the other is the right reading.) The second rejected
stanza occurs just before the stanza beginning " They'll turn me
in your arms, Janet," etc.,

> My right hand will be gloued, Janet,
> My left hand will be bare ;
> And these the tokens I gie thee,
> Nae doubt I will be there.

230

(line 26) " A rose but barely three."
(line 27) " When up there started him, young Tamlaine."
(line 28) " At lady Janet's knee."
(line 38) " And by the grass-green sleeve ; "
(line 40) " At her he spar'd nae leave."   ED.]

BONDSEY AND MAISRY.

I have followed Buchan for this ballad, adopting from Scott only a stanza or two.   Here for once Buchan's version is both shorter and purer than any other I have seen.

THE BONNY HIND.

Copied from Scott, with the corrections given by Motherwell. Herd was the first to take down this admirable poem from recitation.   The greatness and perfection of it stand out still clearer when set by the side of " Lizie Wan "—a rougher tho' still noble version of the story.   Buchan's ballad of " Castle Ha's Daughter " is a later and feebler form of " The Bonny Hind " worth reference, but hardly worth transcription.

THE EARL OF ERROL.

This rather singular poem is historical in subject, but by treatment belongs decidedly to the very rare and valuable class of ballads in which I have ranged it.   Buchan, Sharpe and Kinloch have published versions of it ; mine is chiefly taken from Kinloch.   Buchan, probably from a mistaken idea of congruity, has given only an emasculated text of the ballad before giving it a place.   His note on it, however, as well as Kinloch's, is very curious, although not very quotable.   " Here " it concludes, " I must let the curtain drop . . .   I would not offend modesty ; for Semiramis, Queen of Egypt, could not have said more than did Lady Errol on her husband's trials."   For the two last lines of the first stanza as it stands here and in Buchan, Kinloch reads :—" The apples they grow red and white, And the pears

He tappit the ba' then with his foot
And catched it with his knee,
And through and through the Jew's window
He garr'd the bonny ba' flee.

He's done him to the Jew's castle
And walk'd it round about,
And there he saw the Jew's daughter,
At the window looking out.

"Throw down the ba', ye Jew's daughter,
Throw down the ba' to me!"
"Never a bit, says the Jew's daughter,
Till ye come up to me."

Thus in Sir E. Brydges' fragment, varying slightly from Percy's first stanzas :

It rains, it rains in merry Scotland,
It rains both great and small ;
And all the children in merry Scotland
Are playing at the ball.

The following stanzas are all that appear to me worth notice among those which could not be included in my text :

A schoolboy walking in the garden
Did hear him groan full grievously ;
He ran away to the deep draw-well
And fell down on his knee.

Says—" Bonnie Sir Hugh and pretty Sir Hugh,
I pray you speak to me ;
If you speak to anybody in this world
I pray you speak to me.

(This latter stanza is twice repeated afterwards by the mother.)

" Put a Bible at my head, he says,
And a testament at my feet ;

The earth and worms shall be my bed
Till Christ and I shall meet."

(Motherwell " And pen and ink at every side,
            And I'll lie still asleep.")

" Now Lady Maisry is gane hame,
Made him a winding sheet,
And at the back of merry Lincoln
The dead corpse did her meet.

And a' the bells of merry Lincoln
Without men's hands were rung ;
And a' the books of merry Lincoln
Were read without man's tongue ;
And ne'er was such a burial
Sin' Adam's days begun."

Before I thankfully rid myself of this drudge's work of pick-
ing out stanzas to be sewn together and ticketed, I may add
that many of these verses just quoted would have been simply
thrown into the text, if the one version had not been so generally
incongruous with the other, or if the poem could have been
increased in length without suffering in its effects. Some indeed of the stanzas given are as beautiful as almost to make
tolerable the base labour of annotation and collation.

BONNIE BAHOME.

A fragment of this ballad is in Jamieson, and a full but corrupt
copy in Buchan. Rejecting the absurd or futile stanzas to be
found in each, I have endeavoured to complete my version by
the help of other fragments found afloat on the chaos of Buchan's
book, encumbered by incongruous and unlovely admixture of
base matter ; these I have left exactly as they were, not thinking
fit to correct even the evident corruptions " sea and side."
" water and side." The two or three last verses have been
appended to at least one other ballad, originally published by

Maidmart, but seem to me as well placed here. There is so
much beauty and interest in detached verses of this ballad
that I have taken some pains to give it in a better form than it
was before current in.

[The original reading " Clerk " for " Lord " in these stanzas
was cancelled, except in the 12th, by Swinburne when he revised
the ballad.—ED.]

JOHNIE OF BREADISLEE.

My copy of this noble ballad is chiefly taken from Scott's,
corrected by Kinloch's and a little enlarged from one of the two
fragments first published by Mr. Fry. Kinloch's version is
called " Johnie of Cocklesmuir " ; a fragment given by
Motherwell, containing stanzas to be found in Fry and Kinloch,
" Johnie of Braidisbank," and Fry's two versions (first properly
divided by Mr. Child), " Johnny Cock." The latter of these
opens thus :—

> Fifteen foresters in the braid alow,
> And they are wondrous fell
> To get a drop of John's heart blood
> They wad sink a' their souls to hell.
> Johnny Cock has gotten word o' this
> And he is wondrous keen ;
> He's casten aff the red scarlet
> And on wi' the Linkum green.

Further on :—

> He's tane a horn out frae his side
> And he blaw baith loud and shrill
> Till a' the fifteen foresters
> Heard Johnny Cock blow his horn.
> They hae sworn a bloody oath
> And they were all in one,
> There was not a man amang them a'
> Would blaw such a blast as yon.

Neither fragment gives the wonderful stanza preserved by Finlay :—

> " There is not a bird in a' this forest,"

but the following two stanzas instead of it ;

> There is not a wolf in a' this wood
> Would have done the like to me ;
> She'd have dipped her foot in the cold water
> And sprinkled alone my ee ;
> And if I would have waked for that,
> Would have gone and let me be.
> (v.l.-And gin that would not have done,
> Would have gane and let me be).
> But fingers five save me alive,
> And faint heart fail me nought ;
> And silver strings, value me sma' things
> Till I get a' this vengeance wrought."

Scott's version is by far the completest, though I think touched a little here and there with modernisms ; no other genuine text that I know of gives any conclusion at all. In Scott the main body of the ballad is also more perfect and clear ; but the most beautiful of the stanzas here inserted are gathered from the fragmentary copies I have classed above.

YOUNG REDIN.

Scott and Kinloch have given the best versions of this ballad ; but Scott's text is seemingly interpolated and Kinloch's defective. The lost or cancelled stanzas I have supplied from Buchan's version, a full and valuable one, though as usual, something the worse for wear, especially at the opening. Two of these various readings I add here ; the one Kinloch's, the other Buchan's.

> Young Redin's till the hunting gane
> With thirty lords and three,
> And he has till his true love gane
> As fast as he could hie.

"Ye're welcome here, my young Redin,
For coal and candle-light;
And sae are ye, my young Redin,
To bide wi' me the night."

" I thank ye for your light, lady,
Sae do I for your coal;
But there's thrice as fair a lady as thee
Meets me at Brandie's Well."

Lady Maisry forth frae her bower came,
And stood on her tower head;
She thought she heard a bridle ring
The sound did her heart good.

Another version reads:

She heard a sound of bridle reins
She wished might be for good.

She thought it was her first true love
Whom she loved ance in time,
But it was her new love hunting,
Come frae the hunting of the hind.

For the two last stanzas I have gone to Buchan's text, not
without a doubt whether Kinloch's were not better. It is here
given that the reader may choose for himself.

Then they've made a big bane fire
The bower-woman to brin;
It tookna on her cheek, her cheek,
It tookna on her chin,
But it took on the cruel hands
That put young Redin in.

Then they've tane out the bower-woman
And put the lady in;
It tookna on her cheek, her cheek,
It tookna on her chin,
But it took on the fause, fause arms
That young Redin lay in.

For keckle-pin (heckle-pin, the tooth of a flax-comb or heckle as the glossaries translate it) Scott reads " hollin green," which is not improbably right. His version has much in it that I have had to leave out, preferring the story as given by later editors. All the authentic copies published of this ballad are given carefully and faithfully by Mr. Child in his third volume, where the reader, if he likes, may hunt up the differences of texts.

THE CRUEL MOTHER.

Of this glorious ballad there are about as many versions as verses. I have followed very closely that of Buchan, correcting it by the briefer texts of Herd and Motherwell, which have supplied a few insertions and alterations. I subjoin all the various burdens with which the ballad has been recited. Mother-well's is :—

> Three, three and three by three ;
> Three three, and thirty three.

a burden of such singular beauty that I had almost adopted it in preference to Buchan's, and resigned it at last not without a keen regret.

Kinloch's is :—

> All alone, and alonie ;
> Down by the greenwud sae bonnie.

Mr. Aytown's is :—

> Ah Welladay !
> The wind gaes by and will not stay.

A late version also given by Buchan and called " The Minister's daughter of Newark," alters Kinloch's burden to :—

> Hey wi' the rose and the lindie O,
> Alane by the green burn sidie O;

Most of the readings in this text were weakened copies of the first ; but towards the end it has a valuable passage not in

people in escaping. And indeed in the present case the supreme worth of the poem on all grounds must be so evident as to excuse any labour spent in resetting all scattered and broken pieces of it.

CHILDE WATERS.

I have adopted the South country version of this ballad given by Percy in preference to the various Scotch texts, as being both older and better than any form under which the poem has since appeared. The form, manner and language of a southern ballad are so curiously unlike those in use on the border, that Childe Waters must naturally seem out of place in a collection such as this. Notwithstanding on comparing it with " Burd Ellen " and " Lady Margaret " in Jamieson and Kinloch it appeared so evidently superior that I could not well have preferred any other version.

LIZIE WAN.

This ballad, apart from its own great merit, is interesting compared with "The Bonny Hynd," as giving a similar story cast in rougher type and more broadly tragic in incident. In the other two ballads which touch upon the same matter the note is of a higher pitch throughout, and the language more delicate and careful. Nevertheless, in spite of its brusque abruptness of style, " Lizie Wan " is a valuable poem. The two last stanzas occur with slight differences in " Son Davie " and " The Wood o' Warshir," but it is clear that here at least, they are rightly placed. " Lizie Wan " seems to me pure and incorrupt in language and has, apparently, been very little altered ; if at all, I should say by omission and compression. Herd first published it in his second edition ; I know of no latter collection in which it has found a place.

[There are two manuscript copies of this ballad. The first we quote. In the second, the only differences occur in

the suggested substitution of " felon " for " fallow " and in
the following variants :—

> " and I'll tell you a reason for why "   (line 6).
> " and I can shew you why."   (line 14).   [ED.]

THE QUEEN'S MARIE.

Except in two stanzas I have followed Scott's version of this
ballad all but exactly ; I add such various readings only as
appear to be of real merit.   Motherwell in place of Scott's 4th
stanza reads :—

> The Prince's bed it was sae saft,
> The spices they were sae fine,
> That out of it she could not lie
> When she was scarce fifteen.

Instead of the stanza beginning

> " Queen Marie came tripping down the stair,"

which is taken from Motherwell, Scott reads :—

> Scarcely had she lain down again,
> And scarcely fa'en asleep,
> When up then started our good queen
> Just at her bed-feet ;
> Saying " Marie Hamilton, where's your babe ?
> For I'm sure I hear it greet."

I may just add that for " rings " in the stanza referred to other
versions read " strings " and " links."   The stanza beginning

> " What need ye heck ! and how ! ladies ? "

is taken from Kinloch.

Upon the whole I think there can be no question as to the
infinite value of Scott's text when set by the side of any other.
Not in mere choice of words and metrical power only, but in
the tone of the whole poem, it is far superior to the many
versions since published.   There is a stateliness and completion
in it which we miss at once in the pathetic vulgarisms of Kinloch
and Motherwell ; of Buchan, as of latter editors, I say nothing.

That this great ballad relates to Mary Stuart and Darnley

there is of course no doubt; but its actual basis of fact seems of the loosest. A French chambermaid and an apothecary are the culprits brought forward by Knox.

WILLIE AND MAY MARGARET.

I have followed Buchan almost literally for this ballad, in preference to Jamieson and Aytown, whose version is comparatively modern and imperfect. Here, as in " Bondsey and Maisay," Buchan's text, torn and spotted as it is here and there by wear of time and corrupt recital, preserves the original type and body of the poem better than that of a more precise and critical editor.

LONG LONKIN.

The more usual title of the ballad is " Lammikin," but the name turns up in every fresh version under some novel form of corruption. My text is based mainly on the ordinary texts of Jamieson and Aytoun corrected by a valuable fragment by Child from Richardson's " Borderer's Table-Book." In a ballad so constantly recited the various renderings are of course infinite; many of the extant versions being base and modern.

[In a note at the end of this ballad Swinburne remarks that " the usual version of the stanzas describing Lonkin's entrance is as follows :—

> But the nourice was a fause limmer,
> As ever hung on tree;
> She laid a plot wi' Lammikin,
> When her lord was ower the sea.

> She laid a plot wi' Lammikin
> When the servants were awa',
> Loot him in at a little shot window
> And brought him into the ha'.

> O where is a' the men of this house, etc." ED.]

PART I

ADDITIONAL NOTES

THE YOUNG TAMLANE.

In Scott's Minstrelsy this ballad is preceded by a long discourse on the "fairies of popular superstition."

THE JEW'S DAUGHTER.

Percy suggests that the subject of this ballad was probably founded upon an Italian legend. Mirryland Town was thought to be Milan Town.

JOHNIE OF BREADISLEE.

Kinloch in his "Johnie of Cocklesmuir" repeats the last line of each stanza as a kind of burden; Swinburne follows the example of Motherwell and omits it.

THE KNIFE IN THE SHEATH.

This has the title in Motherwell's collection "The Broom blooms bonnie and says it is fair." [ED.]

PART II

NOTes

BURD MARGARET was probably suggested to Swinburne by Jamieson's " Burd Ellen " and Buchan's " Lady Margaret."

THERE GOWANS ARE GAY. Buchan has a ballad entitled " The Gowans sae gay " and Prof. Child has a similar ballad under the title of " Lady Isabel and the Elf Knight." (Vol. I).

LORD SCALES although bearing a slight resemblance in its final lines to the ballad entitled " Lord Randal " in Jamieson's " Popular Ballads and Songs " (Vol I, p. 162), is quite different and must also be distinguished from the " Lord Randal " of Scott's Minstrelsy.

THE WORM OF SPINDLESTONHEUGH recalls the theme of "Kempion" or "Kemp Owyne." See Buchan and Motherwell.

LORD SOULIS is the title of a ballad in Scott's Minstrelsy ; in the same collection there is a " Lyke-Wake Dirge " and " The Lament of the Border Widow," which no doubt inspired Swinburne to write his " Lord Soulis," " A Lyke-Wake Song," and " The Tyne-Side Widow." The " Widow's Lament " by Thomas Smibert or " The Widow " by Allen Ramsay may also have been suggestive for the last named ballad. [ED.]

LADY ISABEL.

" I have seen no version of this ballad but that in Buchan, which is lax and unequal. As it has some beauty, and as the story is original and not without interest, I have given it a place, omitting the last stanza in Buchan as needless, ugly and common by way of conclusion to many modernised ballads." [A. C. S.]

There are two mss. of this ballad. The second contains the following alterations :—

Line 10 "As white as the lily flower ; "

Line 13 " Mother."
Line 48 " That is prepared for me."
Line 52 " This woman's prepared for thee."
Lines 53-56 are missing.
Line 71 " a brooch."
Line 72 " a ring."
Lines 79-82 Slowly to the bower she came
                 And slowly enter'd in ;
                 And being fu' o' courtesie
                 Says—" Begin, mother, begin."
Line 89 " rosy lips "
Line 96 " Amang the angels fine ;

In place of the last six lines the second Ms. reads :

                 " Nae moan was made for Lady Isabel
                 In bower where she lay dead ;
                 But a' was for that ill woman,
                 In the fields mad she gaed."

EARL ROBERT.

(Four lines deleted between the 9th and 10th stanzas).

                 Gin I may win to ye, Annie,
                 I think ye'll keep me well.
                 I were the liefer of you, Robert,
                 But for the doors of shut steel.

                                                          [ED.]

PART III

NOTES

A JACOBITE'S EXILE, A JACOBITE'S FAREWELL. These ballads may have been inspired by the "Jacobite Relics" of Hogg.

THE KING'S AE SON. There is a mention of an "ae son" in Scott's Minstrelsy ("Prince Robert.")

MAY JANET. In the first series of "Poems and Ballads" these verses are described as "Breton" but the ballad has no connection whatever with "Breton" folk-lore.

Jenny or Janet was a favourite name in Border balladry. There is in the ballad collection of Robert Gilfillan, the title "Janet and Me," while Swinburne himself in "Lord Soulis" has the line,

> "Out then spake May Janet's brother,"

Janet is also a name in "The Young Tamlane." [ED.]

GLOSSARY

Abene (to let abee)   to let alone.
ahint   behind.
aik   oak.
aith   oath.
aits   oats.
arow (arrow)   angry.
ask   newt.
awry   uneven, distorted.

bale   beacon-fire.
bauld   bold.
bearing-bread   bread used in celebration of a birth.
ben   inner room.
bent   open field ; coarse.
benty   covered with coarse or dried grass.
bidene   suffering, bearing.
bigged   built.
billie   love.
birk   birch tree.
bout   leap, spring.
boun   ready.
bouted   sifted.
brake   fern, thicket.
brast   burst.
bree   eyebrow.
brigg   bridge.
brittled   killed and cut up.
broo   broth.
burd   maid.

busk	to deck, dress.
but and	and also.
caitive	captive.
carknet	necklace.
carle	old man.
carlie	little man.
carline	old woman.
cavils (to cast)	lots (to cast).
champaign	open country.
chuckie-stanes	small stones used in a game.
claith	cloth.
cledding	clothing.
cleek	iron hook.
clerk	clerk.
clip	to clasp.
clout	patch ; mend ; strike.
cod	cushion or pillow.
coft	bought.
coil	bundle of hay ; noise ; fuss.
colled	cut obliquely.
corks	cork heels for shoes.
crack	to chat ; boast.
craw	to crow.
creel (creil)	basket or hamper.
croup	to make a hoarse noise.
dail (daill)	intercourse.
dang	flung.
daubing	shame ; smearing.
daw	to dawn.
dead	death.
den	valley.
ding	to kill ; overthrow.
dole	doxy.
doo	dove.

dool	*see* "dule."
douk	to dive, search for.
dowie	dreary, melancholy.
drae	to draw.
dree	to pine, endure.
drumlie	dark, foreboding.
duddies	tatters.
dule	sorrow.
eebree	eyebrow.
eke	to add to, to lengthen.
esk	*see* " ask."
erlish	ghastly.
fallows	fearful.
farder	further.
fee	wages ; (adj. predestined ; on the verge of death).
fell	crag, field.
fey	unfortunate.
filed	defiled.
filing	defiling.
fleet	to float or flow.
flour	floor.
flur	to scatter, fly up.
flyting	scolding, brawling.
forbye	beyond, aside.
fordone	exhausted, ruined.
gad (of **airn**)	bar of iron.
gair	*see* " gare."
ganging	wandering.
gar	to make, cause.
gare	a piece of cloth inserted in a robe.

garth	a meadow.
gate	way, gate.
gay	pretty.
gear	spoil.
gin	if.
gowan	wild daisy.
gowd	gold.
grathed	dressed.
greet	to cry, sob.
grewhound	grey hound.

ha'	hall, manor house.
halse	to embrace.
halse-bane	neck bone.
halp	to help.
hantle	much; a considerable number.
hap	to wrap up from the cold or rain.
hasp	to fasten with a cloth.
haud	hold.
hawse	to embrace.
heal	to conceal, defend.
heck	to pant.
hinny	honey.
hirtle	to run or walk as if lame.
hollin	holly.
honey-brap	drop of honey; term of endearment.
hooly	gently.
how	to tarry; linger.
howk	to dig; burrow.
huly	slowly.

| intill | into. |

| kane | tithe or tribute paid by fairies and witches to their master the devil. |

keach	catch; commotion.
keckle-pin	tooth of a flaxcomb.
ken	to know.
kell	net work; film.
kevil	*see* " cavils."
kilt	to tuck up.
kirtle	gown.
kist	a box; chest.
knappies	knobs.
laidly	loathly.
laigh	low.
lauchter	lock of hair.
lane	alone.
lear	learning.
leeland	grass-land; open or untilled ground.
leman	lover.
liefer	rather.
lig	to put down.
lily	yellow.
lin	ledge.
ling	thin long grass.
loun	rascal, rogue.
loup	to leap.
lout	to stoop.
lyke-wake	a watch over a dead body.
maik (make)	companion, match.
malison	curse.
mane (to make a)	to complain, lament.
marl	earth or clay used as manure.
may	maid, girl.
maw	to mow.
mealpock	beggar's mealbag.
mean (to make)	to moan, lament.

mend	expiation, atonement.
mickle	very much.
mirk	dark.
moanand	groaning.
mool	soft earth.
mote	stain.
mould	earth, grave.
muckle	great.
muir	moor.
musk	moss.
neist	next.
nether	lower.
ower, owre	over.
owsen	oxen.
pall	any fine or rich cloth.
pearlin	kind of lace.
pike	to pull out.
pile	tender blade, twig.
pillow-bere	pillow cover.
pine	pining.
pore (por)	hole caused by sword, or knife thrust.
prim	to pin up hair, etc.
prink	to deck.
propine	power of giving.
published	proclaimed.
quit (queet)	coat.
rank	heavy (rain).
rape	rope.
ravelled	entangled.
reck	track or trace.

rede	counsel.
rig	ridge or path.
rine	to touch ; ditch.
roup	to make a hoarse sound, to cry.
routh	abundance ; plentiful.
row	to roll.
sabelline	sable.
sained	hallowed, blessed.
scaith	damage.
scale	dismiss, spill, scatter.
scart	breeze.
scoup	to accompany.
scour	to clean by rubbing.
scrogs	stunted trees.
seen (seyne)	sinews.
— (seyn)	consecrated parts.
selle	saddle.
sendal	thin silk or linen.
shatwindow	low window or one opening outwards and upwards.
shaw	wood.
shearing	reaping time.
sheen	to shine.
shouther	shoulder.
siccan	such.
side	hanging low.
siller	silver.
sing	to singe.
slae-thorn	black-thorn.
sowm	to swim.
spale	wooden cup.
spar	to bolt (in "Wearieswa"—made of)
spate	flood.
speir	to ask, question.
spoke	bar.

spune	spoon.
stand (of milk)	vessel containing milk ; stall.
stark	strong.
streek	to lay out a dead body.
straik	stroke.
syne	afterwards.
tauld	told.
tane (the)	the one.
teen	sorrow, anger.
teind	*see* " kane."
thae	these.
thairben	inner apartment.
thairbut	outer apartment.
thole	to suffer, bear.
thretty	thirty.
tirl	to turn the handle of the latch.
tow	to pull.
twal'	twelve.
twine	to part, sever.
tyne	to lose.
unco	unknown.
vails	servant's gratuity.
vair	kind of fur, squirrel's skin.
vervein	plant accredited with efficacy in love.
wa'	wall.
wad	pledge, wager.
waefu'	pitiful, woeful.
wale	to choose.
waly	alas !
ware	to expend.
warsle	struggle.

wean	child, infant.
web	covering.
weed	dress, clothes.
weel-faured	good-looking.
ween	to fancy, boast,
weet	wet.
weird (wierd)	fate, destiny.
whin	gorse, furze.
whinstone	hard stone, toad-stone.
wide	to wade.
wight	swift, courageous.
win	to proceed, arrive.
wonneth	to dwell.
wonning	dwelling.
wot	to know.
wrask	vengeance; anything oval-shape.
wrade	kind of seaweed.
wyte	blame.
yett	gate, door.

LADY MAISIE'S BAIRN.
Lady Maisie's Bairn and Other Poems, printed for private circulation, 1915.

A FRAGMENT OF A BORDER BALLAD.
Poetical Fragments, 1916.

WEARIESWA'.
Printed for private circulation, 1917.

THE EARL OF MAR'S DAUGHTER.
Posthumous Poems, 1917.

BORDER BALLAD.
A Lay of Lilies, 1918.

L.